LIGHT WHEN IT COMES

LIGHT WHEN IT COMES

Trusting Joy, Facing Darkness,
and Seeing God in Everything

CHRIS ANDERSON

WILLIAM B. EERDMANS PUBLISHING COMPANY
GRAND RAPIDS, MICHIGAN

Wm. B. Eerdmans Publishing Co.
2140 Oak Industrial Drive N.E., Grand Rapids, Michigan 49505
www.eerdmans.com

22 21 20 19 18 17 16   1 2 3 4 5 6 7

ISBN 978-0-8028-7399-6

Library of Congress Cataloging-in-Publication Data

Names: Anderson, Chris, 1955–   author.
Title: Light when it comes : trusting joy, facing darkness,
      and seeing God in everything / Chris Anderson.
Description: Grand Rapids : Eerdmans Publishing Co., 2016. |
      Includes bibliographical references.
Identifiers: LCCN 2016028012 | ISBN 9780802873996 (pbk. : alk. paper)
Subjects: LCSH: Christian life—Catholic authors. | Spiritual life—
      Catholic Church. | Ignatius, of Loyola, Saint, 1491-1556.
Classification: LCC BX2350.3 .A53 2016 | DDC 248.4—dc23
      LC record available at https://lccn.loc.gov/2016028012

For the people of St. Mary's

Contents

....

CONTENTS

PART III
SEEING GOD IN EVERYTHING

Paying Fierce Attention

....

Yet again once again I am in a classroom of seething bubbling grinning headlong small children, and we get to talking about miracles and God and gods and how words like "God" are all webbed and hoary with history and meaning and opinion and blood, and are there other words for the things that we are hinting at when we say words like "god" and "miracle" and "reverence"?

And off we go, to the teacher's astonishment (she is sitting politely in the corner with a look I know all too well, a mix of Is this a good idea? and Lordy, they sure seem into it), talking about how all living things have the spark of holy somehow, even hornets, and how maybe the spark gets blown out somehow, like in terrorists, and how maybe just paying fierce attention is the most eloquent way to pray, and how there are so many things for which we don't have words that mean much, words that do anything more than affix a small label to the incomprehensibly vast and crucial, that we easily forget that the things are quite real, and not merely ideas. Like love, for example, I say. You need love like food, like water, and if you don't get it and give it you'll wither and get smaller and meaner and brittle and eventually your skin becomes a prison in which you live alone, wailing.

We talk about how religions are useful at their best but murderous corporations at their worst, and how religions are probably best thought of as clans and tribes and guilds and languages and vocabularies and compasses and houses in which you know the layout so well you could walk around barefoot in the dark and not stumble once. We talk about how there are all sorts of illuminated beings in every sort of context, and how some beings serve their fellows by being great listeners, and others have healing hands, and others are good at getting everyone to come to a disgruntled agreement about the direction of the voyage, and others are terrific mothers and fathers and aunties and musicians and clowns and dancers and builders and fixers and teachers and learners, and how some beings are lucky to discover that their skill, their gift, the thing they love to do and do really well, is to pay fierce attention to the holy of everything, to notice the flourish and song of holy and the awful of bruised and broken holy, and report on this to their brothers and sisters, which is, of course, everyone.

Such people in the ancient Irish tradition from which I came, I tell the children, are called seanachies, which means story-catchers or story-sharers, and their job is really important, because stories of grace and courage and humor and love and wild tenderness are compass points and lodestars, and if we don't catch and share stories that matter, we will have nothing but lies and blood, and can't we do better than that? Isn't that why human beings were given the extraordinary gifts of imagination and humor, to try to put lies and blood out of business after millions of years? Isn't that why?

After a while we went back to talking about noses and crickets and bears and pears, and eventually I shuffled home, but I have been thinking about that classroom ever since, and I think the book in your hands is that burbling classroom, and that its author is a seanachie, and that he pays fierce tender attention, and that you will be illuminated somehow when you read what he saw, what he sings of the holy everywhere around us, even hornets.

Brian Doyle

Preface

....

Maybe whatever seems
to be so, we should speak so from our souls,
never afraid, "Light" when it comes,
"Dark" when it goes away.

—William Stafford

The shock of stars at five a.m. The bright belt of Orion and the arc and sweep of those other brilliant, nameless lights and even the blackness glittering.

The smell of wood smoke and fir. The cold, damp air.

I hear the voice of my wife calling from another room: "Do you know where I put my book?"

Standing at the sink rinsing out a bowl, I look up and see a strand of a spider web rising and falling, made visible by the wind. Then another and another, looping from the willow to the roof. Glinting on and off. As if all the shingles and boards of the house are secretly bound with thread.

We all have moments like this, moments that move us

somehow, that seem to mean something we can't quite put into words, but we are embarrassed by them or we doubt them or in the rush of things that happen to us each day we forget about them. For a moment we believed—in something—a presence, a beauty. But we let the moment pass.

"The believer," Pope Francis says in *The Joy of the Gospel,* "is essentially one who remembers."

My purpose in this book is to help you remember the moments, and to trust in those moments, to believe in them, by sharing moments from my own life, as a husband and father and grandfather, a teacher of English and a Catholic deacon. "I have said these things to you," as Jesus tells his disciples, "so that my joy may be in you and your joy may be complete." However small they are, however fleeting, moments like this can lead us to God.

And not just the moments of joy but the moments of loneliness and struggle and fear. Darkness is important, too, and in a way more important, because it is darkness that teaches us the nature of light. In darkness, too, God is calling us.

This is the idea of the *examen* of conscience, the much-loved prayer of St. Ignatius: that God is always calling us, that the Spirit is always moving in our lives. The *examen* is a simple but powerful way of remembering, and I mean the scenes and stories that follow to be examples of how it works, how it keeps deepening and opening up.

At the end of each day:

> *we remember the light and give thanks for the light;*
> *we remember the darkness and ask for forgiveness, and*
> *   refuge, and strength;*

*and we let it all go: we ask for the grace to follow the light,
to know what we should do—but then we leave it all to
God, trusting in his kindness.*

The light of grace is always shining, it's always pouring
down, though it's refracted and scattered and easy to miss,
and so one way to pray is to look back on the moments of our
day and recall when we saw the light breaking through, and
when we didn't, when we felt it being blocked or opposed.

This is the practice of joy: remembering.

And then releasing—waiting, too, for an idea to form or
an intuition to emerge about what God is calling us to do, but
waiting with the knowledge that these things are mysteries, beyond understanding, and trying to give up our need for control.

The moments are poetry, not prose. We are rarely given
a single, clear message, an unmistakable sign, or at least a
message or a sign we can explain in the abstract. The practice of joy is the practice of scene and the practice of story,
because joy is an experience, not an idea. The best we can
do is describe what happened.

The moments are parables. The details are simple,
and yet there's something "arresting" about them, as C. H.
Dodd says of the details in a parable. We glimpse something,
we encounter something, and yet we are left in "sufficient
doubt" about what the image means or the details point to
that we are "teased into thought," just as we are by the stories Jesus tells.

The root of the word "parable" in Greek is *paraballo*,
to place one thing beside another, to juxtapose, and this is

what Jesus does. He puts images side by side. He leaps from one idea to the next. He brings things together and asks us to bring things, too, connecting what we can and accepting what we can't—accepting everything.

Be not afraid, Jesus says. The light comes and the light goes, and all we have to do is see that and name it.

We don't have to resolve the tensions, and we don't have to reconcile the opposites, and we can't. All we can do is live with things the way they are, trusting the days to God— remembering the darkness and remembering the light, and holding them both in our hearts, together, side by side. Our only obligation is to speak what is so. Our longing. Our grief.

The stars and the web.

The voice of the one we love, calling from another room.

PART I

TRUSTING JOY

The first movement is singing.
A free voice, filling mountains and valleys.
The first movement is joy,
But it is taken away.

—Czeslaw Milosz

CHAPTER 1

Seeing the Light

I am called to bless a bathroom.

A young poet has committed suicide there. Her boyfriend found her and tried to revive her. He was soaked with blood when the EMTs arrived, and then the police, and though he's moved out now, and the biological hazard team has scrubbed the blood away, the landlord and the boyfriend and the boyfriend's father want some kind of further cleansing, maybe a kind of magic. But who am I to say?

So I drive to the complex, a warren of condominiums, chalky and cheap, and I wander around until I find theirs, and I knock on the door and introduce myself to the parents—fifties, disheveled, in dirty sweatshirts and jeans—and they take me down the hall, past boxes and piles of clothes. The condo is new, the bathroom small and bright.

I squeeze in by the toilet, stand against the wall, facing the mirror, and say the prayers for the dead and the blessing for a house, my voice echoing, and with a small, plastic bottle begin to sprinkle the room with holy water. The vanity. The mirror. The clean, fiberglass tub. *Perpetual light shine upon her, O Lord. Amen.*

The boyfriend couldn't bear to come. His mother and father stand in the doorway, bowing their heads.

And as I wave the bottle and say the words, the cap flies off, it pops, bouncing into the bottom of the tub, and I have to lean over to get it, picking it up off the slick, shiny surface of the fiberglass. *May she rest in peace*, I say, embarrassed now, but alert, too. Aware. The words as they echo in that hollow place sound good to me, and proper, and true. *May the souls of all the faithful departed through the mercy of God rest in peace.*

Then I turn, trace the cross in the air, and give the final blessing—in my left hand the cap, about the size of a dime, with a hole in the middle. Like the prize in a box of Crackerjacks. A whistle, or a top.

The old woman in ICU wants to rail against the church. *Patriarchy*, she says, *hierarchy*, and I sit and listen.

"But you're dying," I say. "Why are we talking about this? Why does any of this matter?"

And the sun slants through the dusty window. My Roman collar chafes. On the monitor, the peaks and valleys of her failing heart.

"May I give you communion?" I ask her. And she says, "Would that mean I'd have to come back to the church?"

"No," I say. "No. It will be our little secret."

Are these moments of darkness or moments of light? Both, and neither. I would call them moments of joy, because joy, as C. S. Lewis says, isn't just pleasure and isn't just happiness. It's deeper than sadness and deeper than grief but contains them, holds them.

All I have done is come into a room—a bathroom, a hospital room—and I have been awkward and clumsy, and there's been something odd about the moment, and random, and embarrassing, and yet I also have this sense of privilege, of being accorded some high honor.

Something solemn is going on.

———

God doesn't come to us in a wind, and God doesn't come to us in an earthquake, and God doesn't come to us in a fire. God comes to us in a still, small voice, as he comes to Elijah in the first book of Kings. All we have to do is listen.

Jesus is always walking towards us, on the water—and we are always jumping out of the boat, in our joy—and when we feel how hard the wind is blowing, we always sink, as Peter does in the story in the Gospel of Matthew. And the wind is the wind of doubt, the wind that blows from the culture we live in, a culture that tends to ridicule religion, that tends to reduce the mystery. And that doubt is in us, too.

Maybe, we think, Jesus didn't really multiply the fishes and loaves; he just inspired the people to share the food they'd brought. Maybe Jesus didn't really rise from the dead; the people just lived new lives in memory of him.

And so we explain the Bible away. We turn every miracle into metaphor, draining the Scriptures of their power and meaning.

Not that we have to prove the miracles happened in some obvious way. That's another kind of reduction, a reduction to the merely physical, as if God were a magician who can only get our attention through special effects. Sure, he can. He can do anything. But why would he stoop so low—

especially when it usually doesn't work? The people in the Gospels witness these astonishing things, they see these miracles, and in the end they kill Jesus anyway.

"God did not dictate the Scriptures word for word," Robert Barron says. "Rather, God spoke subtly and indirectly, precisely through human agents who employed distinctive literary techniques and who were conditioned by the cultures in which they found themselves." The Bible is the Word of God, but filtered through human language and reflecting human limitations, and part of what this means is that we have to figure out what kind of writing we're reading. We don't watch *The Lord of the Rings* the same way we watch *Apollo 13*, *The Simpsons* the way we watch *Restaurant: Impossible*, and it's the same with the Bible. It's full of different genres—songs, histories, tall tales, dialogues, letters.

And a gospel—a "gospel" is a special kind of writing, not the news but the "good news," carefully shaped, faith-filled history, based on eye-witness accounts and then arranged with an awareness of pattern and image and form to convey not facts but faith. It's not a biography of Jesus. It's a joyous affirmation of belief in him.

The point isn't to reduce the idea of miracle, but to expand it. The point isn't to drain the Bible of its power, but to show that this power is present in our time, too, in every moment.

In Jesus the difference between matter and spirit has been forever transcended. What's miraculous isn't the walking on water but the water itself, the lake, the Sea of Galilee, thirteen miles long and eight miles wide, with the sun rising over it in the mornings, and every lake—Yellowstone Lake and Lake Pend Oreille and even Cronemiller Lake, the pond in the woods by our house in Oregon—because God is everywhere, lovely in ten thousand places. The miracle is life itself, the ordinary.

This is why we come to church: to offer up these moments, to consecrate them and so become more aware of them, to give thanks for them.

Jesus didn't just live, he died, and he didn't just die, he rose, and he didn't just rise, he ascended, and then he sent the Holy Spirit, which is flowing through the universe and has always been flowing through the universe, from the beginning of time.

Everything is miraculous.

The seed really falls into the earth, and the fields are really smooth and bare, and then the rain comes, and the sun, and the leaf and the grape, and then the crushing and the wait, the long wait for whatever it is enzymes do.

Water is always becoming wine.

My wife, Barb, and I were driving through the fields and hills, and I looked out at the trees and the new-cut hay, at the farms as we passed them, and for a while I felt an unusual peace, a sense of happiness and blessedness. Deeper than usual. Quiet but intense. I can't put it into words. I didn't even tell Barb about it. We talked about ordinary things. We listened to music. But for a while, an hour or more, I had this quiet sense of joy, of belonging, as if some kind of energy was flowing into me from somewhere else.

But not *as if*. An energy *was* flowing through me.

Thoughts like this are not *our* thoughts. They are the

still, small voice; they are Jesus coming towards us, on the water. Sure, we'll jump out of the boat and sink, again and again. We're all like Peter. These moments pass, and we doubt them and then forget them. We're embarrassed to talk about them. That's OK. Jesus reaches down and pulls Peter out of the water, again and again, and we just have to accept that about ourselves, our limitations, and believe that about Jesus, his forgiveness and persistence.

And besides, the water is fine. Even in our drowning, the Lord is with us. The water is clear and sweet, and the light is shining through it.

———

The image in Jeremiah, in the New Jerusalem Bible's translation, is the "Watchful Tree." When the Lord first comes to Jeremiah, he comes with a question: "What do you see?" And Jeremiah answers, "I see a branch of the Watchful Tree." And the Lord says, "Well seen, for I am watching over my word to perform it."

"Watchful," *sheqed*, is the Hebrew name for the almond tree, the first to bloom in the spring. The almond tree is the Watchful Tree because we watch for it, we wait for it, as the first sign that spring has come again.

I walk into a room, and the woman I meet seems to give off light. Something is glowing inside of her, maybe an emptiness, and it leaks out the corners of her eyes.

I walk into a room and I sit down by a man, and there is a darkness inside him, a meanness. I seem to see a sheet of oil, sliding down a pane of glass.

This is the work of the *examen*: to remember the darkness and to face it. To remember the light and to follow it.

I go to visit our old sacristan, who always used to dress to the nines. Tweed skirts. Silver hair just so. But now she has lost her mind, she is demented, and I go over to the assisted-care facility to bring her communion, carrying the consecrated host in a small, silver pyx.

She welcomes me formally. "Won't you please sit," she says, then calmly peels off her housedress, over her head, like a girl—right there, in front of me—and stands before her closet, in her slip, deciding what to wear.

I had brought Christ into that room. She knew she had to change.

I'm talking with a friend and he says, "The older I get, the less my faith is *bound*." I think he means bound by religion. Bound by dogma and creed.

Not me. The older I get, the more I need the small, the tender spaces. The circle of light by the tabernacle. The statue of Mary beneath the Japanese maple.

Her head is bowed. Her hands are open. In spring the buds leaf out.

"I am only a man," as Milosz says. "I need visible signs. . . . / I tire easily, building the stairway of abstraction."

———

Just a shape at first, wide and blank, merging with my own dark outline on the road, the shadow of a hawk passes over my shoulder, so suddenly I flinch, I start, as if some unexpected hand has touched my actual body.

But gently, without a sound.

Seeming to dissolve then and rise, becoming three-dimensional: a sparrowhawk, golden, gliding just before me along the curve, a single feathered muscle pushing off finally above the fields. Behind it, in the delicate sky, bulging in air, as huge and sudden as a world, the afternoon moon.

———————

When, walking in the woods, I pull out my long black rosary, the beads loop down and jingle a little like the leash when I pull it out to put the dogs back on. And the dogs, when they hear it, come running up, heads cocked, tongues lolling.

No, I say. *It's OK.* And they bound away again.

———————

When some of us say God has spoken to us or we believe in Jesus Christ, we're using a kind of shorthand for a sequence of leaps and decisions that begins in our own experience, in our joy and sorrow and need. Some people actually see Jesus himself, even now, or hear his voice. I believe this happens, this kind of direct revelation, but it doesn't seem to happen very often, and for most of us it never does. For most of us "the Lord is my shepherd" or "He guides me in right paths" are phrases we decide to apply to subtle, everyday things.

One day we are overcome with a feeling of well-being. Reading a book, we suddenly understand something we didn't understand before. Over time, a conviction starts to build in us. We walk by a river or hike in a forest or look at the people we love, and we have this nameless sensation, this feeling beyond words.

Except we do name it, some of us. We do give it words. Because of our upbringing and our tradition and our life in the church, we label this experience with a dogma, we describe it with the words of the creed, we understand it through the Scriptures. We've made a leap.We've moved from the concrete to the saving abstraction. We say, This feeling, this glimpse of something beautiful and meaningful and real—everything that everyone else experiences in the course of their daily lives—this is Christ. We reason from the gift to the giver, from effect to cause.

In the ninth chapter of John, Jesus heals a blind man. He spits on the ground and makes clay with the saliva and smears the clay on the man's eyes. Then, after telling the man to wash in the pool of Siloam, Jesus walks away. When the blind man is healed and the people ask him how it happened, he has no idea. All he knows, he says, is "I was blind, now I see."

It's only later, after the experience, that Jesus returns and asks him, "Do you believe in the Son of man?" "Who is he, sir? Tell me, so that I may believe in him." Jesus says, "You have seen him, and the one speaking to you is he."

In the fourth chapter of John, when Jesus encounters the Samaritan woman at the well, he doesn't lecture her first. He talks to her. He drinks the water. Then, in the context of that particular, human experience, that gradual dawning of understanding and joy, he gives the experience a name, he tells the woman who he is, and she accepts this. She believes. "Come," she says to the townspeople. "Come and see a man who told me everything I ever have done!"

Jesus tells us our lives. The story of Jesus and the teachings of Jesus make sense of what we experience every day. They reveal its underlying meaning. And so we believe. First the well, then the creed. First the hot, dusty day. Our deep thirst.

———

The Word of God is a seed, Jesus says. And the thing about a seed is that it's hidden, in the earth. It's buried. It takes a long time to grow, and at any point in the life cycle of that seed you might stand there and look and not see a thing.

To say faith is like a seed is to say it is a process, a journey, a way of life, not an idea you can grasp once and for all. To say faith is like a seed is to say there are seasons of faith. It comes and goes, it ebbs and flows, and you don't understand or have control over it, any more than a farmer can control the sun and the rain, however hard he works. To plant a seed is to surrender. You can't make it grow.

Adam falls asleep in the Garden, as we must fall asleep. It's good to be awake, it's good to use our reason and our minds, but reason can only take us so far. Finally, to get deeper, to get closer to the mystery, we have to let go of our ability to shape and control and analyze, and surrender, fall, deep into the realm of the unconscious, where we can be one again with creation and with ourselves. Faith isn't a matter of concepts or numbers. It's a matter of love.

And the first words that Adam speaks? God has created a woman while Adam slept, formed her from one of his own ribs, and Adam wakes up, and he looks, and he sees, and his first words—the first recorded words of the first man—are poetry.

This at last is bone of my bones
and flesh of my flesh.

It's poetry that gets us closest to the mystery, because in poetry there's something that can't be translated out; in poetry the imagination and the feelings speak.

It's parable that gets us closest to the mystery, because the details of a parable leave us in "sufficient doubt." They "tease [us] into thought," pointing beyond themselves to what can never be spoken, only heard.

The Kingdom of Heaven is a like a man who sowed seed, Matthew says. The Kingdom of Heaven is like a treasure buried in a field. This is what there is. There are treasures. There are seeds. Moments.

The Kingdom of Heaven is like the room in your dream and outside is a lake so blue and cold you know something big is about to happen.

Then you wake up and have your coffee and don't think about the dream again.

The Kingdom of Heaven is like writing fast and not leaving anything out, and the same idea that always forms starts to form again. You know it's just an idea, you know you're just floating on the surface of reason, but underneath you feel something big pushing up from the dark.

The Kingdom of Heaven is like when you're walking on the docks and your best friend from high school sees you a hundred yards away and even after all these years knows it's you. "You have the same walk," he says. "You lean the same way." All this time this man was alive and you were, too, and you didn't think about each other for decades, and now he takes you in his boat to the other side of the lake, and his wife is making Jello and the cabin is full of pots and pans and dog-eared books he has read and reread just like you. All those cabins in the trees! All those roads winding out to highways and cities you've never been to, with offices and neighborhoods and parks where kids are throwing footballs.

Walking up the little valley. Morning. Heavy dew. Suddenly a field of spiders, a field of webs, every thistle strung like a racket.

The Kingdom of Heaven is like the ecology of your yard. All these animals are scurrying around and building nests and entering into all these conflicts and alliances, just like in a Walt Disney movie or a book by E. B. White. And you never see them usually, maybe a squirrel now and then, a bird, but you never give them a moment's thought, never think about them at all, until one morning you walk out the door and nearly step on a headless mouse, eviscerated, heart and lungs spilling from the breast. Another gift from the cats, another sign of their prowess.

Those shiny viscera on the welcome mat. Those intricate systems, inside out.
That dark red heart, like a coat of arms.

CHAPTER 2

Doubting the Light

.

"My mind to me," Augustine says in *The Confessions*, "has become a piece of difficult ground."

Sometimes my mind to me becomes like the sound system at church that week it was picking up the morning talk shows.

The priest would be invoking the Spirit to come upon these gifts to make them holy, or we'd be saying the Our Father or the *Agnus Dei*, or there'd be one of those silences we really go to mass for, one of those moments when we're sitting in our places and we can hear the silence of all of us being together and rustling and breathing in this big space smelling of candle wax—and all the while some AM talk-show host or another would be gibbering in the background, mumbling over the speakers, softer, then louder, blah-blah-blah-ing. We couldn't understand what the words meant. We just knew they were words; we just recognized their jagged, spiky syntax, because it's always in our ears. There's a radio talk-show host in all our heads, a pale, bloated, spitting man blithering on and on about who to hate, most of all ourselves.

O God, my mind to me has become like a sound system. It has become to me a piece of difficult ground. It has become to me like the stream this morning and the trees along the stream and the warblers hopping from branch to branch in the trees, the Townsend's Warblers and the chickadees, fretting the bare maple and oak. I was walking down the road, and it was muddy and wet, and the Townsend's Warblers, with that soft, yellow almond curving around the dark of their eyes—they're back, they're making their way again. And standing on the altar behind the priest, later, at mass, stepping forward to raise the cup, I suddenly realized this. This came to me with a start. The warblers are back, and I had already forgotten them.

Several years ago I spent thirty days on the Oregon coast on a silent retreat. I lived in a hut above Nestucca Bay and tried to do the Spiritual Exercises of St. Ignatius. Following the structure as best I could, I meditated on the Scriptures and journaled four or five times a day. I met with my spiritual director every morning, and I walked a lot and talked to myself, and I tried to discern the will of God for me.

This is when I first practiced the *examen*. What light had I glimpsed in my life? What darkness had I failed to face? What question was God calling me to live?

And I thought I was going to go out of my mind. I hadn't realized how addicted I am to the roles I play and the titles I have, or to television, or to thinking.

And it was a wonderful time, too. I hadn't known God existed. Not really. But then I reached out and touched the bark of a tree and felt something like electricity passing through me, up from my feet through the top of my head, and it felt like tears and it felt like grief. I fell asleep and dreamed, and in the dream I fell in love. I watched the clouds form and the weather come in. I watched a Swainson's thrush lift up its head and sing. I read the Scriptures and saw my own face as in a mirror.

The Psalmist cries out:

The hills gird themselves with joy,
the meadows clothe themselves with flocks,
the valleys deck themselves with grain,
they shout and sing together for joy.

Jesus didn't drive an SUV. Jesus didn't text and Jesus didn't Skype and Jesus didn't have a microwave. There were always animals looking through his windows, their eyes like small, brown planets, and there were fields and hills outside his door, and he was always walking in them.

From the Mount of Beatitudes, above the Sea of Galilee, you can see in one view the places Jesus taught and healed and gathered his disciples before he went to Jerusalem. You could walk it in a day, from Magdala to Capernaum, and that's part of the point—that people walked in the first century, that in the region of Galilee there weren't even very good roads for horses and chariots. We are called to be like Jesus, to imitate him, and like everyone else in those villages, he walked seven to nine miles on an ordinary day, on his own two feet, one step at a time, slow enough to see the flowering mustard and hear the mourning doves and stop and talk to the people who sought him out.

"There's no smallness anymore," a friend said to me as we stood there, looking out at the water and the sky.

The Incarnation could have happened anywhere and at any time. God could have chosen to come into history in

Ohio in 1955 or in 555 in Japan, or he could have decided to wait until the twenty-third century and come on another planet. But he didn't. He chose to come into one small and lovely landscape, and in a time before technology had so sped things up we'd lost the ability to see and to feel.

It's not just that we're supposed to love and honor the birds of the air and the flowers of the field. We're supposed to be like them, Jesus says.

Don't worry about tomorrow, he says in the Sermon on the Mount.

Be here. Be now.

———

The summer after the Thirty Days I came back to the hut above the bay. Everything was soft and beautiful. I could see the water through the alder and the elderberry, and the warblers and the thrushes moved in the branches, and on impulse, I picked up my cell phone and left myself a message.

I just felt the urge to talk to somebody, and I knew my wife was gone that evening. So I called myself at the university—I'm not sure why—and when I heard my own brisk, professorial voice asking me to leave a message, I did. I felt foolish, but I did.

Summer went by. I went to my first long, dispiriting meeting of fall. When I walked into my office again, I was already tired and depressed.

I sat down in my chair, picked up the phone, and began to check my messages.

And there, from the past, from high above the water of

the bay, was my other self. I'd forgotten. I hadn't thought about the moment among the trees, in the evening light. But there it was again, and there was my voice, my other voice, sending a message into the future, and it sounded so gentle and so wise it was like the voice of someone else.

Remember: You are loved.

———

Praying in my sadness a decade of the rosary, bead after bead along the chain, I look over the rooftops, through my office window, and see a giant crane swinging out its arm. The tower must be ten stories tall, the boom another ten stories long, counterbalanced, and the sweep of that great latticed arm is so high and stately and slow, I am heartened, I am glad.

How steady the long, smooth glide. Unerring.

I don't even know what they're building. I don't know what hangs from the cable the boom suspends. A girder? A section of wall?

Or maybe nothing. Maybe nothing at all.

On the birthday of the French philosopher Foucault, who thought language was just a tool for crowd control, I walk down the hall after class, in a surge of students, carry-ing a snorkel and a mask.

It's also the birthday of St. Teresa of Avila, who said, "Do whatever most kindles love in you."

And when I get to the crinkly blue water of the pool, in the campus gym, and I slip on my mask and clasp the snorkel in my mouth, then push off from the edge, face down, I am weightless and I am floating, and my legs and my feet lift up behind me as I move, and I suck and I blow. I suck and I blow.

With every stroke I take, I hear the bubbles rising. A silvery trickling, like a brook.

———

One day on our pilgrimage we went to the River Jordan and to the bend in the river where the baptism of Jesus may have taken place.

This was in the desert, and on either side of the road we went down there was a barbed-wire fence warning us about the danger of unexploded landmines.

And as one member of our group stood in the shallow, muddy water, she looked up and saw a white dove descending from the sky—an actual white dove, in the sky above the Jordan—and she was filled with joy and the presence of God.

Later, back home, I had the privilege of baptizing a man my age and his four grandchildren, three handsome little boys and a bald baby girl with a bow in her hair. When the grandfather kneeled at the edge of the fount in the back of church, and I put my hand on his back, and he leaned over, and I baptized him with my other hand, *in the name of the Father, and of the Son, and of the Holy Spirit,* I could feel the Spirit moving in me. In all of us.

Jesus didn't need to be baptized. He is the creator of all rivers, and the creator of all waters, the creator of everything, come now to this one ordinary river, in the desert, and I think he did that in part to show us what we need to do, but also as a way of once again diffusing his spirit through the world. In his baptism, says an ancient Church Father, "he sanctified the fountains of waters" and "into the fabric of miracles he interwove ever greater miracles." It's as if in entering the River Jordan, Jesus recharges with his love and his light all rivers and all waters and all places and peoples forevermore.

At the river the Father's voice comes from heaven, and the Son comes up out of the waters, and the Spirit, like a dove, comes down upon him. And it's through the Spirit we are freed from history. What happened then happened—it did, we can believe it—but Jesus died, and he sent his Spirit, and through that Spirit and in that Spirit what happened then is always happening. Every land is the Holy Land. Every moment is pilgrimage.

In moments like this we are taken out of ourselves, the way John the Baptist is, caught up in something greater than we are. But at the same time, because of this, we find ourselves—our true selves. In losing who we are, we discover who we are: beloved sons and beloved daughters. In this sense we are like Jesus himself in this scene in the Gospels. He comes to the Jordan to tell us again that deep down we are good, we are fundamentally good, made in the image and likeness of God.

It's no accident that in the next scene in the three Synoptic Gospels—Matthew, Mark, and Luke—Jesus is tempted by Satan in the wilderness, because this is how the life of faith is: up and down, the high moments immediately challenged by doubt and fear. The word *Satan* means "the Accuser," and what the Accuser accuses us of is being a fraud. We all have this voice inside of us, this other spirit, this darkness, telling us we're not good enough the way we are, that we should be ashamed of our nakedness. This is how we can discern if we're having a genuine religious experience: the voice of God, of the Spirit, is always the voice of joy. Of self-confidence, even in our humility. The voice of Satan is the voice of self-loathing. Of self-doubt.

Or the root meaning of the word *devil*: "the divider." He who divides us from our confidence.

Yes, we have these experiences, but then they're over, they're fleeting. It's no accident either that the Holy Spirit is often symbolized by a dove or some other kind of bird, because birds fly away—we only glimpse them, we have no control over them, we usually can't capture them and hold them. And so Satan says, Look, that moment wasn't real. It's over now. This—this lonely, painful life—this is all there is.

And in Mark's version of the story it's only Jesus who sees the dove. Luke and Matthew suggest that other people see the Spirit descend, in some form—John, that John the Baptist does—but not Mark. For him this is an interior experience, inside of Jesus alone, as these experiences are almost always interior for us, not something other people can see or verify. "Just as he was coming up out of the water," Mark says, "*he saw* . . . the Spirit descending like a dove."

And the Spirit descends *like* a dove. It's not a real dove. The dove is a metaphor, an image, and you know what our culture thinks about metaphors: they're worthless. You can't buy one.

But the gospel is always the gospel *according to,* as Lawrence Cunningham puts it. According to Mark. According to Luke. According to you and me.

It's like what happened to me once when I gave a talk on faith at OSU, and I poured myself out talking about these experiences I had had of the presence of God. And the first question from the audience, from a professor in another department: *How do you know you're not deluded?*

Because the Lord of all came to the river, and in coming to that river he blessed all rivers. Because these moments don't happen just once. Because these signs are not given just once. They are given again and again, they happen over and over, if only we have the eyes to see them and the hearts to feel them.

In the flight of a dove above the barbed-wire fences. In the little girl with the bow in her hair. In her grandfather, kneeling by the water.

———

Now and then in steady rain a roof vent pings like a cell phone.

Rain glugs in the gutters like the Metolius glugging and gliding over smooth river stones, pouring down from Wizard Falls.

All night the darkness flows above me.

———

At morning mass a garbage truck starts and stops just beyond the sanctuary, the squeals and groans of the compression brakes like the songs of whales, like humpbacks, calling from the deep.

———

Once I was helping my dad move a piano. We were trying to get it down the stairs into a basement. I was on the upper end, barking my shins as we bumped it down. Dad was below, on the heavy end, trying to do it all as always, sweat beading, tendons cording with the effort to wrest that whole black piano down that narrow, impossible passage.

As I let it go. As I had to.

You know how it is when you're trying to move something down a flight of stairs and you're on the upper end. It's hard to keep control. And Dad wasn't waiting for me anyway, he was really carrying it all himself, and he was strong, strong enough to shoulder the weight the rest of the way to the bottom.

What I remember is how slowly the piano pulled away when I first let it go. Like a great ship casting off for icy waters.

———

Jesus doesn't listen to Satan in the wilderness, despite all his flattery and enticements. He rejects him three times in Matthew and Luke: he doesn't turn the stones into bread, he doesn't throw himself from the parapet, and he doesn't take control of the kingdoms.

Jesus is the great non-listener.

Jairus's daughter has died, and the crowd is anxious to tell Jesus the bad news. You think you're special, Jesus? Forget it. You're too late.

But, Mark tells us, Jesus "disregards the message." He goes ahead with what he was planning to do. "Why do you make a commotion and weep?" Jesus asks later in the story. When I walk into a room, I'm easily influenced by what people seem to be feeling. If they're anxious and angry, it rubs off on me. But when Jesus asks about the noise and the fuss, he's saying it's all really meaningless. He's shutting it out. No matter how much people "ridicule" him, no matter how strong the resistance, he's not listening.

Whatever is flashing on my computer, the sun is shining. Breath is coming in and out of my lungs. Whatever is flashing on my computer is usually about the future, and the future hasn't happened yet. The only place I can be is the moment. Everything else is an abstraction. Everything else is, in some fundamental sense, unreal.

Because the issue isn't really not-listening, of course. When I say Jesus doesn't listen, I mean he really listens—but not to the powerful, not to the prestigious, not to those the world regards as important. He listens to the hemorrhaging woman, in this same story in Mark. In all that surge of people he can feel her presence, and he turns to face her and see her. He pays a deep and radical attention to her, this woman the people regard as unclean, as unworthy—and he can do that because he hasn't allowed himself to be distracted by the babbling crowd.

The snowy head, the black wings.

An eagle—a bald eagle—skimming the trees at the edge of town.

And I was startled, I was thrilled, before my little Honda carried me away, before the news on the radio and the tasks of the day blotted out the thought of it—an eagle, soaring over the rooftops, and I forgot.

By the time I pulled into the driveway, it was gone from my mind.

The story of our lives isn't the story of the things we make and the things we do. It's the story of what we've been given to see. To love. To praise.

"God did not make death / and he does not rejoice in the death of the living," the Book of Wisdom tells us, "for he created all things so that they might exist; / the generative forces of the world are wholesome." This is the pattern and this is the rule: we are fundamentally good, and the world is fundamentally good—animated by a creative, "generative force"—and anything that tells us otherwise, any crowd, any individual, is to be shut out and ignored.

The voice of deep or defining self-doubt: that is never the voice of God.

⁓

I know a woman whose husband died and whose son came to the funeral—her estranged son, a son who had pulled away from the family and lived a life many might disapprove of. In fact, several people at the funeral did disapprove, and they let the mother know. What the mother felt was joy at his return; what she felt was a mother's love. But her friends said, That's Satan tempting you, this desire to embrace him, because he's sinful. He's going to hell.

But the gospel says, *Disregard the message. Forget the commotion.*

It says, *Listen to love. Always listen to love.*

———

A yellow warbler in a willow, *sweet-sweet-sweet sweeter-than-sweet*. A marsh wren in the cattails, hacking like a broken sprinkler.

Shivers and gurgles and runs, in the treetops, in the low brush, finches and cowbirds and Virginia rails. A song sparrow: *maids, maids, maids, put on your teeea kettle-ettle-ettle!*

Wait, our guides say, *listen*, and we stop and cock our heads.

It's too wonderful, this knowledge—we can't take it in because it's hidden, and it's everywhere, deep in the leaves, a whistle, a trill, a rush, quick, here-now, then gone.

What we long for we never see. What we love flies away. We stop, and we look where our guides are pointing, into the ash swale, into the oak scrub, like pilgrims in the Holy Land, contemplating the stones: *Jesus was here.*

———

Downstairs in his room my son is playing harmonica with Bruce Springsteen. He doesn't know how, he can't play a note, but he likes to keep time to his Springsteen CD by blowing and breathing, and he's doing that now, over and over, like beating a drum, while inside the downstairs chimney the mother swift has returned to the nest she built in the chimney crook, wings whirring and shuddering for a moment as if the furnace has come on.

She built the nest there last year, too, raising a brood, but I forgot to put a cap on the chimney, and now she's back, circling the roof before taking aim and dive-bombing exactly to the point, down the chute, out of all the oak and maple and the wide clear summer sky picking out and boring down my own single chute into the darkness of the basement, to the crook where the chimney bends and the chicks wait in their grassy beds.

One second I believe in God, the next I don't. Once I was driving home past the high school, and I looked out at the hills behind the school where the forest begins. It was evening, and the stars were coming out, and all at once I was aware of the great soft shoulder of those trees and hills, as if something huge and gentle had lain down on the earth. Everything came clear. For several seconds I believed in God, completely.

Night coming on and the shoulder of hills and the clear line of the horizon; God lying down on the earth and sighing, with his back to me; God lying down and sighing and going to sleep. It was like a door opening a crack and the darkness starting to pour through, the rich and velvet dark, though it also seemed like light pouring out, white light, before the door whicked shut again.

Then it was over, before I reached the stop sign on Lewisburg Road. I turned and saw the oak on the right, the one where the enormous lower branch broke off in the snow-storm, gashing the trunk open, and the feeling was gone.

The mother swift: how she dives into the opening from the sky above the roof, circling first, then folding her wings and falling, like threading a needle, her body just the size of the bore, almost too big, brushing against the sides as she drops. Then in the basement the whirring of her wings as she hovers to the nest.

And the chicks peeping now! Underneath, the tiny peeping of the chicks.

And my son playing the blues, my son huffing and hacking as Springsteen rasps from his room, huffing and hacking, though he doesn't know a note.

Or just the same note. The one note. Over and over.

CHAPTER 3

Following the Light

If there were an earthquake and you were on the moon look-ing down, you wouldn't see any movement at all. The earth would seem to just hang in space, seas a deep blue, clouds creamy white.

And it's good to look at life like this, from a distance, because it humbles us and exalts us, and it makes us aware of how fragile life is, and interconnected, the way it did the astronauts, gazing homeward through their hatches.

But it's good, too, to zoom in and keep on zooming, from high up all the way down to the very pixel you're in, to the liv-ing room and to the couch in the living room and to the little dog sleeping on top of the back cushions of the couch, his head and his front paws draped over your shoulder in such a way that one day during Holy Week, when in the scene from the Last Supper in the Gospel that morning the Beloved Disciple leans back in his love and his sadness and his grief against the chest of Our Lord, your left ear is pressed against the chest of that little dog, and you hear through the layers of his fur and muscle and bone the steady beating of his little doggy heart.

You sit there a long time. You hold very still.

Imagine the house where Mary grew up, St. Ignatius

says in one of his spiritual exercises—his favorite one, tradition says. Imagine the house of Mary, the Mother of God. The cool stone walls. A basket on a shelf:

> *I will see, in imagination, the great extent and space of the world, where dwell so many different nations and peoples. I will then see particularly the city of Nazareth in the province of Galilee, and the house and room where our Lady dwells.*

This is how we learn to follow the light: by thinking first about "the great extent and space of the world," but then zooming in. Narrowing.

Mary shooing away the chickens. Mary going to the well. Mary standing at a window in the morning light.

I first received the Eucharist in the shabby living room of the bungalow near campus where we were housesitting for a professor on sabbatical, a few of us gathered around the coffee table, among shelves of jumbled books. Dave falling asleep. Our jumpy Irish Setter mix biting Katie on the palm and Barb having to take her to get stitches, though I didn't learn about this until later, as I didn't learn many things.

Peter was the celebrant, the young Jesuit who talked with such ease and economy about Hegel and Sartre and Camus. How I loved those ideas. How I loved those beautiful structures.

But as I look back now, the process of my conversion feels more like a matter of being carried along by moments and of living in the moment. I don't remember the raising of the host or any of the words. I remember the dusty sunroom off the porch where in the evening we used to sit and

watch *Masterpiece Theatre.* Or sitting on the edge of the wa-
terbed one summer morning as I was waking up, sitting for
a moment and looking down at the orange shag carpet and
rubbing my face with my hands and feeling my face in my
hands and thinking, *This is me, this is my body.*

———————

This is how we learn to follow the light: by choosing to
respect our moments of "consolation," those moments in
the *examen* when we feel heartened and strengthened and
calmed.

Most of us are taught that the negative always cancels
out the positive, the gentle and the good are illusory, the vi-
olent and the ugly real. But St. Ignatius makes the opposite
assumption:

> *In time of desolation one should never make a change, but
> stand firm and constant in the resolutions and decision
> which guided him the day before the desolation, or to the
> decision which he observed in the preceding consolation. For
> just as the good spirit guides and consoles us in consolation,
> so in desolation the evil spirit guides and counsels.*

Don't trust your depression and don't trust your confusion,
Ignatius says. Admit them, face them, but recognize they're
not who you are. You are made in the image and likeness
of God, and so whenever you are happiest and most alive,
that's when you will feel and know the will of God.

Should we get married? Should we take this job? If we
feel good as we imagine the possibility, if we feel at peace,

consistently, over days and weeks, as we do the *examen* and reflect on the light and reflect on the darkness, this is the direction we should try to go, this is what we should do, unless something practical gets in the way or we'd have to forsake some necessary responsibilities to go there.

———

This is how we learn to trust the light: by moving from the head to the heart.

After dinner J. R. R. Tolkien and C. S. Lewis are walking out on the lawns at Oxford, where they both teach. It is September of 1931. Lewis is on the verge of becoming Christian, and Tolkien is trying to help him take that last, difficult step.

Your problem, Tolkien says to his friend, is that your imagination isn't strong enough. When you read the great stories of literature or the fairy tales you love, you allow yourself to be swept up and swept away. But when you come to the stories of the Gospels, you become "narrow and empiricist," as Lewis remembered in a letter to a friend about this crucial moment in his life. Your imagination shuts down, and you start asking all kinds of rational questions you don't ask otherwise.

Here's the key, Tolkien says. The story of Christ should be seen as a story like those other stories, just as beautiful and powerful, and it should work on you in the same way, through your imagination and your heart. But with this difference: this story really happened.

Tolkien and Lewis later turned to the writing of science fiction and fairy tales exactly as a way of stealing past what

Lewis calls the "dragons" of reason. We "freeze" when we come to Scripture, he says. We feel restrained. But "by casting these things into an imaginary world, stripping them of their stained-glass and Sunday school associations," Lewis and Tolkien tried to make the biblical stories "appear in their real potency."

Maybe that lump we feel in our throats when the great Lion returns from the dead is our deepest and truest intuition about God. Maybe we should trust those foolish tears.

———————

In Jerusalem the churches swarm with tour groups, each with its guide, lecturing in low tones about history and architecture. The walls echo with commentary.

But outside the Church of All Nations, at the Garden of Gethsemane, on the Mount of Olives, there is a sign: *Please: No Explanations Inside the Church.* And you walk through the doors, and you sit in a pew, and there is silence, finally, and coolness, and shadows.

The altar is built above a hole where a large, flat rock rises out of the marble floor—the rock where, tradition says, Jesus knelt and prayed the night before his crucifixion, and where you can kneel and pray, too, along the edges, lining up first to bend down and kiss the stone or run your hands over its thick, dark layers.

I don't know.

Maybe we've got it backwards.

Maybe choirs of angels really sing at all the important moments and Charlton Heston's muscles really ripple and shine and everything is shot in Technicolor, rich and thick and bright.

Jesus really kneels in his compassion, and he holds the gourd to Heston's lips, gently. We see this from behind, over Jesus' shoulder—we see the back of Jesus and his coarse, cream-colored robe and his soft brown hair. And Heston looks into his eyes, he looks into the face of the Lord, in wonder, and he drinks of the water, and his thirst is quenched and his load lightened on the long march through the desert to the galleys and his eventual redemption, years later, after the chariot race, round and round the sandy circus, those magnificent white Arabians surging and straining and Heston, teeth bared, snapping and pulling the reins.

Then the *Via Dolorosa* and Jesus stumbling under the weight of the cross, and Heston rushes up and gives *him* water, and again he looks into the eyes of the Lord—and again we see this from behind, we only glimpse the sacred shoulders, naked now and scored—and then the crucifixion and the earthquake and the great cleansing storm, violins and cellos swelling, cymbals crashing. All the graves are opened and all the sores are melted and all the filth is sluiced away.

Everyone is laughing and crying. Everyone knows.

It's only we who are watching who never see his face.

In Galatians St. Paul gives us a checklist of feelings to follow and not follow. We don't see God directly, and we can't be sure of how he moves in our life, not exactly, but we can look inside ourselves and pay attention to what we're feeling, over time, and this is enough, this is everything, because these feelings are effects we can trace back to their causes.

On the one hand, there are the fruits of what Paul calls "the flesh," things like "hatreds" and "rivalries" and "outbursts of fury." Don't follow those. When you write that nasty email, don't send it. When you feel the urge to cut someone off in the parking lot, resist it.

On the other hand, "the fruit of the Spirit is love, joy, peace, patience, kindness, generosity, faithfulness, gentleness, self-control." Practice those. Act on their impulses and urgings. The kind word. The apology. The gift.

As Ignatius puts it, trust your feelings of "consolation." Trust "any increase of faith, hope, and charity and any interior joy that calls and attracts to heavenly things."

Distrust thoughts that "weaken, disquiet, or disturb the soul by destroying the peace, tranquility, and quiet which it had before." Disturbance like this "is a clear sign" that these thoughts and impulses do not come from God.

Diadochus of Photice uses the image of a tranquil sea. When the storms come, the water churns and we can't see into the depths. "The skills of the fisherman are useless." But in the glassy calm we can see all the way to the bottom. "No fish can hide."

Thus we distinguish between the thoughts "that are good, those sent by God," and those that are not.

The good thoughts "we will treasure in our memory."

I walk down to the Humanities Center for a reception. People crowd the narrow rooms, holding plastic plates, drinking wine from plastic cups. I have this feeling of being trapped. Stuck.

But that night it starts to rain, and it rains so hard I wake up and open a window so I can listen to the abundance of rain and the generosity of rain.

The precision of rain: *every* leaf.

———

I stand in my office looking out the window. My door is closed. Below me students walk between classes. And for a moment I have a sense of the presence of Jesus, in the room, behind me.

I hesitate to talk about this. It feels very personal. Very intimate.

What I felt wasn't physical, exactly. It was a presence. But it was the presence of a person, of a man, and of a man with hands and feet and warmth and energy.

The experience lasted just a few minutes, and it was never overpowering, and even as it was happening I was also doubting it and questioning it. But for those few minutes what I felt was a kind of intense and quiet joy, and a lifting of the burden, and a hope.

Most of the time faith is just an idea for us, a set of dogmas we have to work hard to explain. But what if the church isn't just an institution, and the language we use isn't just language, and there's nothing we have to explain or justify? What if Jesus is real, and he's here, and he really does love us?

I was standing at the window, and it was raining, and I had this feeling. Jesus was with me. He was in the room somehow, and in the air of the room, and he wasn't an idea, he was a person. It was almost like my son was standing there, or my father—it was the way you feel when someone you know comes up behind you—and I could feel his kindness, I could feel his awareness of me. His interest in me.

It was like a dream, too. If I turned my head, it would all go away.

I don't know. All I can tell you is that for a few minutes I was no longer worried about the things I had to do and no longer afraid of failing and no longer tired and discouraged. I wasn't thinking about myself at all.

The rainy street below. The students beneath their umbrellas, hurrying along.

———

I fall asleep in a room high above the sea. That night a storm blows in, with heavy rains, lashing the house again and again. Once the wind slams so hard the bed jumps.

This really happens: the frame shudders, then stills.

Sitting in my office talking with a student, I suddenly feel dizzy. It's as if the building is swaying. But then I realize that the building *is* swaying, it's rocking, and the light hanging from the ceiling is swinging back and forth, and it's as if a wave of energy is rippling through the floor—no, *is*.

Sometimes it's not we who move.

If you sit long enough by a window early on a winter morning, you can see the moon set into the dark trees, you can see it sink, very slowly, every minute or so a little further, until finally it disappears entirely, glowing in the tops of the firs.

———

Politely, with all apparent innocence and curiosity, Hank has come to ask about angels. As if I might know the answer. As if anyone would.

Late afternoon, November, my office warm and bright. When I look out the window into the darkness, all I see is my own reflection.

Hank purses his young man's lips, pushes back his young man's hair. His hands are small.

Professorial, I put up my feet and stall: Choirs, Hank, choirs, at least in Dante, everyone flying back and forth and singing—though only metaphor, of course, only image, because all we really know is joy, and only now and then.

Or forests, Hank. Think forests, the deep trees and great trunks. We walk and walk in fragrance and shadow, or I have at least, I have—haven't you? Surely in your life, even in the malls and before the screen, you have felt the brush of what seems like wings? What has swept past you, lifted up? What rush of air?

His eyes are brown, and soft, and small. I think of him as a baby. I think of going home. I think of the bare trees outside and the darkness, maybe stars.

Or the aquarium. Yes. The Oregon Coast Aquarium.

I think of that morning by the huge window cut into the rock where the seals and the sea lions glide past goofy and blissful in the murk and the salt and the joyous buoyant water of the sea like ridiculous soft missiles, like dirigibles, one of them—look at him!—one of them upside down, tiny flippers tight against his blubbery body, eyes closed, a whiskery smirk on his silly, wizened face, improbable as Dr. Seuss. O how they squeeze and glide round that endless tank, aimed and unerring and true, nonchalant, purling and flipping among the pillars with what marvelous virtuosity, entirely weightless and free, veering so close you think they must collide, then curving apart and flying away, up and around that endless, luminous tank like skaters, like clowns.

Maybe it's like that, Hank. Maybe it's like that.

Yes, he says, with a slight nod. *OK.*
But what about the angels? What about the Bible?

I pause, and nod, too. I look at him again.

But I'm thinking of summer, in Spokane. I'm thinking of an afternoon in the garden at Manito Park, and the fragrance of roses, hundreds of roses, Patience and Peace and Double Delight, scarlet and lavender and gold. The lawn is green and smooth. The sun shines down, the bright sun of my youth, through Ponderosa pines. My son and daughter move among the flowers, laughing. O Hank, I wish I could explain how happy I felt among the rows, among the carefully tended legions and ranks of those marvelous soft flowers, or later, in the greenhouse, among the bamboo and the lilies and the honeysuckle, shelf by shelf and row by row. We can smell the dampness and the earth of the pots and the greenness. A little stream runs beneath a bridge, and we stroll within the dome, under glass, in the warm, moist air, and everywhere we look the green leaves and the flowers open out and drop and reach in all profusion and abundance and indifference, overflowing their labels and their pots—indifference, you understand: mindless green joy and push and patience—

Hank is arranging his books now, reaching for his coat.

He has been sitting erect, attentive, but he is smiling now, abstractly, zipping up his backpack.

—like the time, years ago, when my children were babies, in the atrium of a zoo—a milky, translucent, geodesic dome, multifaceted on the outside, and inside, among the palms and the ferns, the birds hiding and singing and sweeping down in their white capes and yellow fans and flaming crowns, feathers spread like sails, like enormous balloons. Some had beaks like nutcrackers, others like wedges of melon. Some sang inside the soft darkness of the leaves, out of sight, though sometimes, if you stopped and waited, perfectly still, they'd brush past you with their wings.

I can't help thinking it was black outside, it was dark, but we were walking within the jewel, we were enclosed, breathing in the air and the steam, and the birds were singing and flying all around us, toucans and cuckoos and parrots, the scarlet ibis, the nightingale, and we walked and walked and never came to the end, never touched the glass of the outer wall. We could have been anywhere. We could have been in space.

PART II

FACING DARKNESS

One does not become enlightened by imagining figures of light but by making the darkness visible.

—Carl Jung

CHAPTER 4

Dying to Ourselves

When my oldest son was sixteen, we drove to Spokane to pick up an old car my dad was giving him, a '69 Mercury Bobcat, rusted along the doors.

The next morning John got into the driver's seat, backed out, grinning, and disappeared down the street on his long way home, 400 miles, by himself, through the desert and the mountains.

All I could do was stand there and watch him go.

"Another word for father," says the poet Li-Young Lee, is "worry."

When I think of the image of God the Father, God the Father of Us All, I think of his sadness. I think of him standing in the driveway, watching his son disappear.

Annie is a first-grader in a town not far from where I live. She was abused by her father, and her mother was abused, too, and finally, before the father left them both, in his anger and his meanness, he burned their house to the ground.

Annie's mother is a screamer. She likes to scream at Annie, and she likes to come to school and scream at the teachers, and now she's living with a new boyfriend, which means that Annie is living with a new man, too.

And one day in class Annie drew a cross. She spent some time on it. The wood of the cross is brown and Jesus, hanging on it, is deep red. And at the bottom, in Annie's awkward printing and jumbled spelling, there's this:

I love God because he died for my sins. He died on the cross. He loves me. He had angels. He is the Dad of the world. His name was Jesus but we call him God.

I don't know how Annie learned about Jesus, what church she might have gone to, but these six brief sentences are profound in ways that she can't understand—or that maybe, come to think of it, she can. Somehow, in the midst of her suffering and the violence and ugliness of her family life, Annie knows of the cross and thinks of the cross, and the cross gives a meaning to her suffering and a meaning to her life.

My God, my God, why have you forsaken me? Jesus cries out, and he means it. This moment is absolutely desolate and absolutely bleak. It is the end of all meaning. And at the same time, it is the beginning.

God is not an all-powerful God who ignores the suffering of others. He is an all-powerful God who by his very nature gives all his power away. He is Absolute, and he chooses to empty himself out, absolutely.

God is dead. The CEO in the Sky is dead. The Great Policeman is dead. The Unwavering Judge is dead. The God we love because he gives us what we want. The God we resent because he doesn't. He has given himself away.

He has surrendered his power and he has surrendered his potency and so we can't blame him anymore, for hunger and poverty and war, for the injustice and suffering in the world. He has a body, an ordinary, fragile body, and now that body has been tortured and beaten and hung up before us.

God is dead and we rejoice. God is dead and so our own life becomes possible, our true life—our life with him, this beautiful, broken man, this beautiful, broken god.

———————————

To pray the *examen* doesn't just mean to revel in the light. It means to face the darkness, too: the darkness of suffering, the darkness of our own limitations.

It's the darkness that shows us the light. It's desolation that teaches us what joy really is.

When the letters of Mother Teresa were published, and they were full of doubt and despair, MSN was shocked: a saint, full of doubt? Lots of people were surprised.

But not the people who had been praying a long time. Not the people who had been walking the path. They knew the saints are always full of doubt. They knew doubt isn't contrary to the tradition: it *is* the tradition.

Lord, my God, Mother Teresa writes to her confessor,

who am I that You should forsake me? . . . You have thrown me away unwanted—unloved. I call, I cling, I want—and there is no One to answer. The darkness is so dark—and I am alone. Unwanted, forsaken. . . . Even deep down, right in, there is nothing but emptiness and darkness.

The word "darkness" appears hundreds of times in these letters. It's Mother Teresa's dominant image. In the beginning, she says, when she first felt called to her work in India, "there was so much union, love, faith, trust." But now that's gone. The sisters and the people around her think her faith must be strong. "Could they but know how my cheerfulness is the cloak by which I cover the emptiness and misery."

And there's nothing unusual about this. This is the way it is, for all the saints and all of us. We start out experiencing sweetness and consolation in prayer, and that's good and to be trusted. And then the desert happens. It inevitably happens. Our moments of joy come and go, and sometimes they just go. If we stick with prayer long enough, we sooner or later enter into periods of desolation, sometimes long periods, years, and many people give up long before then.

And it's not just that. The longer we pray, the more we begin to experience the pain we bring with us. The longer we pray, the more we have to face our emptiness and our need. When God really touches us, Ruth Burrows says, we begin to "shrivel up." We begin to feel like "empty husks."

No wonder we turn away.

More and more churches are preaching the Gospel of Prosperity, and more and more people are joining. The message is simple. If we're righteous, we'll be rich. If we're good, we'll be happy. The problem is that this isn't true, either to the gospel or to the way things are in the world.

In another, heartbreaking letter Mother Teresa talks about a boy who died in her arms. At the end "he was sorry to die because he had just learned to suffer for the love of God." Any gospel that ignores the suffering and dignity of this child is false and arrogant and cruel. Did he suffer because he wasn't good enough? Because he didn't pray hard enough?

But Mother Teresa understood that suffering and pain don't cancel out faith but exist side by side with it. It's never either/or but always *both/and*. The darkness and the light are always side by side.

Or still deeper.

Mother Teresa knew what all the saints know and what Jesus embodied and still embodies—that suffering itself is revelatory, that God is present not just in our joy but in our sorrow.

The prosperous Christians believe because they're prosperous. They think they deserve their good fortune. They think they understand it. But Mother Teresa knew that God is greater than she was. Her doubt only confirmed this. It was exactly because she didn't understand that she understood: God is greater than our joy and greater than our sorrow and greater than all our doubts.

"The Lord is near to the brokenhearted," the Psalm proclaims. He hasn't deserted us. He's died.

God isn't the God who grants wishes, or doesn't, but the Lord of all mercy and the Lord of all hope. All we can do is surrender. All we can do is turn towards the darkness, as we turn a little boat to face the coming wave.

"All deepened life," Friedrich von Hügel says, "is deepened suffering, deepened dreariness, deepened joy."

———

The cross is a lens. It's a standard. It's a way of measuring things. It's our formula for interpreting every situation. What should we do? Whatever conforms us the most closely to the cross. Whatever turns the situation upside down. Whatever reverses our values and assumptions.

What should we do? Whatever empties us. Whatever silences us. Whatever puts us in solidarity with others. Whatever makes us poor. Whatever gives us the chance to die.

———

An old man is dying in a dark, fetid room. His daughter is with him, in her kindness, praying and holding his hand, though he was a harsh and bitter man all his life and abused her and abused his wife. He had been in combat in a war, and maybe that was it, but now he is dying in a dark, fetid room, and he is rigid in his narrow little bed, shaking, hands clenched, and his daughter is with him.

When I come to read the Psalms to him, he seems to recognize the rhythm of the words and how one line is parallel to the next, and this seems to soothe him for a while. He doesn't shake as much. His eyes stop darting back and forth beneath the stony lids.

And later, after I leave, he opens his eyes. He seems to focus for a moment. He seems to look through the darkness at his daughter, and he says two words to her, in a faint, croaking voice: *You bitch*.

Who knows what this man was thinking or what he was seeing. Maybe he wasn't talking to his daughter, maybe he was talking to Death. But this is what he says, *You bitch*, and this is what his daughter does.

She rises from that chair, and she leans over that bed, and she whispers in her father's ear: *Daddy, I love you*. And that night, he died.

Love is a great emptying out and losing. Love is a rising from a chair. It is a leaning over a bed. It is a whisper in a room and a word in a room.

The last thing this man ever said was vulgar and angry and mean. But this wasn't the last thing he ever heard.

Love not only never fails. It always fails. Love is not only patient and kind. It is despised. Love is seen as weak. Love is seen as unmanly. Love puts down its gloves and gets hit in the face. Love never makes a million dollars and never goes viral and never wins the prize. Love has no answers. It doesn't possess the truth but is possessed by the truth. Love is laughed at. Love is made fun of. Love is slapped around and spat on. Love leads us into the desert. Love leads us into loneliness and sorrow.

Jesus died on a cross and he had angels and he loves us. He is the Dad of the World, the father of all of us forsaken by our fathers and forsaken by our mothers, and no one is finally abandoned, no one is finally unloved and unregarded, but everyone is taken up and held in the arms of this cross and in the arms of this man.

———

I am sitting in the Queen of Angels Monastery in Cuernavaca, Mexico. It's Sunday mass, and there is a family next to me, with a girl of about twelve, with very black hair and dark skin, shy at first. Suddenly it hits me how the tables have turned: how this girl I wouldn't have paid attention to at home, this girl I wouldn't have *seen*, this girl I would have avoided, how suddenly *she* is the one with the power. She knows what's happening, and I don't. I don't know a thing.

Then she takes my hand at the Our Father, and we pray— or she does, since she knows the words. Then she turns and offers me the Sign of Peace, smiling this sweet and innocent smile, and I think, What an ass I am! And how blessed.

———

If you struggle in prayer and prayer is hard and you feel lost and lonely and unsure: you're on the right track. You're making progress.

Desolation is a grace, a gift, because it shows us that we're not the ones who make things happen. We're not in charge. Desolation teaches us, St. Ignatius says, that "it is not within our power to acquire or retain great devotion, ardent love, tears, or any other spiritual consolation, but that all of this is a gift and grace of God our Lord." Desolation demonstrates that we shouldn't "claim as our own what belongs to another, allowing our intellect to rise up in a spirit of pride or vainglory, attributing to ourselves the devotion or other aspects of spiritual consolation."

Think of it: How do we know we're not making this up? How do we know it's God we're encountering? Exactly because grace comes and goes. As Thomas Green puts it, paraphrasing St. John of the Cross: "The best proof that it is really God is that he is often absent when we seek him, and present when we are not seeking him." If religion were merely the opiate of the masses, if I were just manufacturing God to make myself feel better, I'd produce him on the spot. I'd make myself joyous all the time.

Desolation shouldn't just humble us. It should encourage us, it should give us strength, because then, when the joy comes, when the idea comes, when the problem goes away, when the sun pours down, we can rejoice and be glad. Because we know: it's not us. We just happen to be here. We didn't plan anything. We didn't do anything. It's the Lord who is sending the peace and the joy. It's the Lord who is with us.

———

Once I shot a bird, a deranged, obsessive junco that had been banging against our window for weeks, fluttering in and up again and again, hundreds of times a day, enraged by its own reflection. You can't reason with a bird. And this one we couldn't scare away, with flags or foil or glittering strips. Nothing worked. After a while even Barb wanted me to kill it.

We woke up Saturday at five a.m. when it started hurling itself at us again, for another day, and she said, *Get a gun.* So I went to a friend of mine, and he loaned me a rifle, patiently demonstrating how to load the birdshot and find the target, and I spent the afternoon stalking through my own back-yard, firing and missing, firing and missing.

It had been forty years since I shot a gun—at scout camp one summer, at the lake, when I got my shooting merit badge. We were the sort of parents who wouldn't let our kids have toy guns, who wouldn't even let them make sticks into guns, though our oldest son became a soldier and went to Iraq and is on his way there now a second time, an expert with an M–16 and a 50-caliber machine gun they call "the saw."

I'd never been on an army base until we went to Fort Benning to watch him graduate from infantry training. We sat in the bleachers like at a football game, and the loud-speakers started blaring "Bad to the Bone," and then these soldiers came out of the woods firing blanks at the crowd through an orange and yellow smoke screen. I was im-pressed at first, I have to admit, though Barb just wept.

What bothered me was that we couldn't tell where he was in the blocks of marching soldiers, later, on the parade ground, all of them sheared and pressed and squared, all of them the same. It was the knob on the back of his head that gave him away, and even then it was like he was older some-how, older and younger at the same time, and in a kind of time warp, too. It was like we were somehow trapped inside a World War II movie. Pearl Harbor had been bombed and we were striking back.

I couldn't shake this feeling. When I finally hit the junco, on something like my fifteenth try—he had flown into a mag-nolia next to the deck, and maybe it was luck or maybe I was getting the hang of it again, but I squeezed the trigger and the rifle fired, and the bird twitched, then dropped, straight down, into the backyard—when I finally hit it, I didn't feel guilty, exactly. I'm not sure what I felt. I know I wanted to get rid of that bird. I know how frustrated I was with the fluttering and the banging. I know how embarrassed I'd been, firing and missing, firing and missing.

Later I drove our four-year-old grandson into town, to the store. I hadn't done this in a long time either. He's our step-grandson. The woman John married before he left for Iraq has two little boys. So we have two instant grandsons, and I'm still adjusting. But it was good to know I could do this still. Strap a little boy into a car seat. Talk to him on the way, looking into the rear-view mirror. Bribe him and pace him and manage him through the aisles of the store as we got our cereal and butter and bread.

On the way home, driving through the fields, I had this feeling that the Honda was very light and that my grandson was light, too. Everything was light. His brown knees. His arms. His sleepy brown eyes.

I thought, When we get back home and I reach in to free him, he'll be no trouble at all. I'll be able to lift him with one hand.

"We have to trust it utterly to God," Ruth Burrows says. "We must be ready to believe that 'nothingness' is the presence of divine reality; emptiness is a holy void that Divine Love is filling."

The *examen* might seem self-indulgent, but it isn't, really. We look within ourselves to make contact with something greater than ourselves.

The *examen* might seem to be just a matter of feeling, but it isn't, really. It's a practice. The challenge is to do it whether we feel like it not, and in fact part of the value of practicing it over time is that it leads us to experience exactly this emptiness, this barrenness, and so to recognize our need for God.

———

When I hear my daughter's voice on the radio, clear and light and true, I think of St. Clare, who is the patron saint of broadcasting, because once when she was ill and couldn't leave the monastery, she saw faint, ghostly images of the mass flickering on the wall of her cell. The raising of the cup. The pious villagers, looking up. She is the patron saint of absence. Of distance.

In Assisi once I saw what they claimed was her ash blonde hair, great, thick curls of it, heaped in a glass box with a golden lid, and I see no reason this couldn't be true, this couldn't be hers, across the centuries. We saw the shoes of St. Francis, too, tiny, like slippers, stained with blood, and the coarse brown habit he wore, and on the mountain, in a cave, the narrow shelf where he slept, curled up like a baby.

There's no telling what it is possible for us to feel.

I think of the day Maggie and I were walking by the track at the middle school—she was four—and before I knew it she was running. She had decided to take off. When I looked up, I saw her in the distance, rounding the curve, her little arms pumping, her wispy hair floating behind her.

As if she was really going somewhere. As if she would ever return.

CHAPTER 5

Holding On

Yelling at my golden retriever on the top of the hill where no one ever goes. Where I can look out at the valley over the fields and mountains. Grabbing the loose folds beneath his ears and bringing his heavy, panting face to mine and shouting, *You idiot dog! You idiot dog!*

When a man appears from behind a copse of trees, out of the blue, with a slight beard and a tight smile.

I look up to see him. I am crouching, red-faced.

Beautiful morning, he says, walking briskly away.

We are called to die to ourselves, but we don't want to.

There is the vastness of the world, but there is also the smallness of sin.

Sin. That off-putting word, with all its associations. But however we name it, whatever the term, there is a darkness inside us, a violence, and sometimes we try to deny it, to hide from it, and sometimes we choose it. We *want* it.

The light is too hard. It asks too much.

———————

Take, O Lord, and receive all my liberty, my memory, my

understanding, and my entire will, all that I have and possess.
Thou hast given all to me; to Thee, O Lord, I return it. All is
Thine; dispose of it according to Thy will. Give me Thy love and
Thy grace, for this is enough for me.

This is the prayer of St. Ignatius, the *Suscipe*, but it's a
hard prayer to pray in the best of times, when we're our best
selves, let alone on most days when we're trying to control
every outcome and determine every moment.

There's an old story about a wise man who went into
the desert to fast and to pray. He wanted to throw himself
into the arms of God. But one day he was walking and he fell
off a cliff. He would have plunged to his death if he hadn't
grabbed a branch partway down.

Hanging by his arms, high above the river and the rocks,
he cried out: *Lord, Lord! Are you there? Help me! Tell me what*
to do!

Let go, came the calm and quiet voice of the Lord. *Let go.*
Seconds went by.

Then the wise man cried out again: *Anyone else out there?*

———

I walk around campus, and I keep hearing the same
story.

"I got so hammered last night," a young man says. And
another: "When I woke up this morning, I didn't even know
who she was." Or I heard a young woman say this, to another
young woman: "Dude, I was on some other level."

These stories are everywhere, we seem to need to tell
them, and I think it's because deep down they're stories

about our thirsting for God. Deep down we really do want to be on some other level.

It's just that often we don't realize this. Our desire is mistaken.

God wants us to feel good—God wants each of us to do what will lead us to joy—but we keep getting mixed up and off track, forgetting what the source of our joy finally is.

I thirst for praise, but praise doesn't satisfy. I thirst for order, but order doesn't satisfy. I thirst for certainty: never to be troubled, never to be confused, never to have to wrestle with things in my mind. But certainty doesn't quench the thirst, and it's not possible anyway. None of this water is clean and pure. None of this water is the living water.

The only question is this: Does God exist, and how do we know? And the answer, as Paul says to the Romans, is that God is in us. "God's love has been poured into our hearts through the Holy Spirit." So it follows: when we feel love, that's the Spirit.

And that's what's going on with the Samaritan woman at the well, in her long conversation with Jesus in the Gospel of John. She knows somehow from the beginning that this man is special. She intuits this, as we often do when we're talking to certain people, and she follows that feeling, going deeper and deeper, and the feeling builds and builds, and finally the woman gets it, she is changed, she becomes joyous and confident and clear.

This water is already inside her. She's had it all along. Everyone who drinks the water from the well, Jesus says, will be thirsty again, but "those who drink of the water that I will give them will never be thirsty. The water that I will give will become in them a spring of water gushing up to eternal life." That spring is in us, it wells up in us, if only we look within ourselves and see it.

Not long ago a study was published in the journal *Science*. Researchers asked a number of college students and people from local churches and businesses to spend between six to fifteen minutes in a bare room without books or smartphones or other distractions and then to report on what the experience was like.

Of the respondents, 57.5 percent indicated that it was difficult to concentrate, 89 percent that their minds wandered, and 49.3 percent that they didn't enjoy the experience. In one experiment over half the men chose to shock themselves with electricity rather than sit there, alone with their thoughts. I'm not sure how this worked, but apparently 67 percent of the men and 25 percent of the woman actually administered a mild jolt of electricity to themselves at least once during their time in the empty room. They zapped themselves—deliberately—out of boredom, I guess, or nervousness. One man shocked himself 190 times.

The problem isn't that God doesn't exist. The problem is that we don't pay attention long enough to realize that he does.

Grace is always falling on us like the rain and the snow that come down, in the words of Isaiah, and the word of the Lord is always going forth, and it comes back null and void only because we've been too distracted to hear it.

There are many moments of emptiness in our lives, too, moments of bleakness, when the birds don't seem to sing.

But unless we let ourselves experience that bleakness, unless we acknowledge that emptiness, we can never admit to our need for grace. The emptiness is the first necessary step. It's a kind of dying, and unless we die, we can't rise.

The ground only looks lifeless and bare. Underneath it, in the dark, the seed is growing. The sadness will give way, if we can bear it for a while. It will open up.

The elderly father of a friend has moved in with her, and at first he was driving her crazy. She's a busy, driven, accomplished woman, she has a lot to do, but her father, though he's in good health, takes a long time to get up in the morning. To put on his slippers. To walk down the hall. He's 86 years old. He's careful. He's deliberate.

And then—this really bothered my friend at first—he slowly starts to makes his tea. He fills the kettle with water. He puts the kettle on the stove. He puts the tea bag in the cup. He gets the milk from the refrigerator. All of this slowly. Carefully.

And then he stands and waits for the water to boil, looking out the window. He notices the birds. He looks at the clouds.

Half an hour to make a cup of tea! I don't have time for this, my friend said.

But then she realized: she does. This is what she's been thirsting for and didn't know it: not the tea but the silence. The awareness.

Jesus heals the ten lepers, and they walk away, and the word that matters in this story as Luke tells it is *realizing*: "As they were going they were cleansed, and one of them, *realizing* he had been healed, returned, glorifying God." As if you wouldn't know you'd been healed of leprosy. As if that wouldn't be obvious.

But we're being healed of leprosy all the time, and we're always failing to realize it. I drive down the road and the leaves are turning yellow and red. A friend says something kind. As I raise the chalice at the doxology, I see the smaller cups reflected, brimming with wine, like rubies in a ruby brooch. But then I let the moments pass, or I never realize they've happened at all.

"God is always a surprise," Pope Francis said in one of his first interviews after his election. "You never know where and how you will find him. You are not setting the time and place of the encounter with him. You must, therefore, discern the encounter."

———

This is exactly the problem. The problem is joy. Is joy itself.

For C. S. Lewis joy is a "technical term" and "must be sharply distinguished from both Happiness and Pleasure":

Joy (in my sense) has indeed one characteristic, and one only, in common with them; the fact that anyone who has experienced it will want it again. Apart from that, and considered only in its quality, it might almost equally well be called a particular kind of unhappiness or grief. But then it is a kind we want. I doubt whether anyone who has tasted it would ever, if both were in his power, exchange it for all the pleasures in the world. But then Joy is never in our power and pleasure often is.

I don't know. I think we often do exchange joy for pleasure.

For one thing, joy doesn't make sense. It's a feeling, and we don't like feelings, and it comes when we least expect it— Ignatius calls joy like this "consolation without cause"—and we don't like that. We like causes and we like effects, and we like causes and effects.

For another thing, joy can't be engineered, it can't be manufactured, no matter how good or smart or disciplined we are. We can do things to increase our happiness or pleasure, but joy is something that just comes, unbidden and unplanned for, and when we reach out to capture it, it disappears. "Joy is never in our power and pleasure often is."

Even in the moment of experiencing it, we only glimpse joy. We don't possess it. Joy is a longing for something beyond us, on the edge, in the spaces between the lines, and in that sense is almost like grief.

The practice of joy is really the practice of the absence of joy. It's the practice of patience. Of trust.

Joy itself can never be practiced. It can only be welcomed. Received.

For a few years when I was growing up, we lived by the river, the Milk River, and our uncle and aunt and cousins came to visit. We kids tore around the yard and played badminton all day, sprawling on the carpet over the Monopoly board at night while the mosquitoes banged against the screens and the grownups talked.

But the last day, even as their station wagon was pulling out of our gravel drive, everyone waving, we walked back inside, and Mom shut the door, and she said, with a sigh, *Whew, I'm glad they're gone.*

I've never forgotten this: the difference between appearance and reality.

Years later, in Spokane, the fall before she died, my father heard my mother shouting from the living room: *Wayne! Come here!* And he came running from the back of the house, heart racing.

It was the moon, rising over the neighbor's roof. A full harvest moon, pumpkin orange. Coming through the front window. An enormous harvest moon, bigger than she'd ever seen before, and brighter.

Bright as a lamp, she said. *A fire.*

In Dostoevsky's nineteenth-century novella *Notes from Underground*, a small-minded civil servant hides in his room nursing grudges against the people who have hurt him. At the end he has a chance at redemption. He's humiliated a young prostitute named Liza, treated her very badly, but for a moment she rises above him and rises above herself and feels compassion for him. She reaches out to him—literally: she reaches out her hand.

But the Underground Man says no, he turns away from the chance for love, and here's why he says he does it:

"Should the world go to hell, or should I go without my tea? I say, let the world go to hell as long as I can have my tea."

This is us. This is us, too.

"Which is better," the Underground Man asks later: "cheap happiness or sublime suffering? Well, come on, which is better?" This is the question at the heart of what Christians understand as sin. Not mistaken desire. Not the failure to follow what feels right or good. It's this, this choice—and which of us hasn't made it? Chosen our tea, or our latte, or the Internet? We'd rather have a cheapness and a shabbiness than the real thing, because the real thing is too much trouble.

There's a sadness we all feel, the comedian Louis C. K. said in an interview with Conan O'Brien. When we just stop and exist in the world, he says, we often feel an emptiness inside us, a nothingness, and we'll do anything to avoid feeling that.

So we start texting, even when we're driving down the freeway, we start fiddling with our apps at eighty miles an hour, even though we know how dangerous it is, even though we know it's wrong.

We'd rather take a life than face our own.

One Sunday, after serving as a deacon at mass, I stand on my own front porch, at home, yelling at Barb.

It's a big, new concrete porch, a half-circle as you walk up to the house, and I'd just washed it off and hosed it down to get ready for company. It looked clean and beautiful. Sparkling.

But then Barb let the dogs out, and they ran through the

flowerbeds and back up to the front door, and there were muddy paw prints all over the place. Everywhere.

So I yelled. I stood there and yelled.

"People will do anything," Jung says, "rather than face their own souls."

———

Grandpa Ted sits at a table in the room I go to, drinking gin from a Mason jar. I didn't know him—he's been dead for fifty years—but it doesn't seem strange to be standing in the kitchen doorway, looking in. He wears one of those white undershirts that don't have sleeves. He needs a shave. His eyes shine glassy and dark.

Once when my mother was a girl she was washing dishes in a wooden sink and a sliver got stuck in her finger. It dug deep into her flesh. But Grandpa's hands shook so hard when he tried to hold the tweezers; he was so bleary and drunk, all he could do was cry. Mom remembers this. How the tweezers shook above her bloody finger. How the tears streamed down his stubbly chin.

Now he sits at a table in the room I go to. It's morning and he's drinking from a Mason jar, skin sallow and damp. I think how frail he is. But then he looks up. His eyes focus. He smiles. He knows me, he knows everything about me, and he wants to say something now, he wants to speak.

So, lifting up the jar with both hands, the gin clear as water, he speaks to me in a voice stronger and deeper than I thought it could be.

Take and drink, he says. *Take and drink.*

———

"Get up and go on your way," Jesus tells the one leper. "Your faith has made you well." The grace is always there. The leper just made the necessary move, the necessary turn.

And if we don't make the necessary turn? "If we are faithless," Paul says, God "remains faithful, for he cannot deny himself." He will never reject us. He won't put us in hell.

We will have put ourselves in hell. We will have already been in hell, a hell we've made, here and now, a virtual hell, an existence in which nothing really happens and nothing really matters and we don't matter, either. We're just here, and we're gone. We shimmer, and we disappear.

———

This is sin: to deny the darkness, and know we have.
This is sin: to choose the darkness.

Peter denies Jesus three times in the courtyard outside the house of the high priest, just outside Jerusalem. He denies his master, his beloved friend, standing in the darkness around a coal fire. The church they've built on this site today, of smooth, sand-colored stones, is called "St. Peter in Gallicantu": St. Peter Where the Cock Crowed.

But we deny Jesus all the time, again and again, in our kitchens, in our offices, in our parishes. Our master, our beloved friend.

We deny Jesus when we turn on a screen rather than endure our own smallness. When we assume the worst about someone else.

We deny Jesus when we fail to speak up for ourselves. When we don't say what we mean. When we let other people tell us who we are.

We deny Jesus when we're too embarrassed to talk about our faith. We deny Jesus when we *do* talk about our faith, but for our own ends, without gentleness or respect.

We deny Jesus when we simplify what is nuanced and complicated and open-ended.

When we do a shoddy job. When we don't make an effort.

When we read the Bible literally, reducing its mysteries to mere fact. When we dismiss the truths of the Bible as mere myth and symbol.

When we expect our parents to be better than we are. Our children to be better than we are. Our friends to be better than we are. Our ministers and priests.

When we fear change. When we fear sickness. When we fear growing older. When we fear death.

When we give up hope—when we give up joy.

Shampooing our golden retriever in ketchup, six in the morning, in the darkness, scrubbing and hosing his skunk-fouled fur, the water pouring down the driveway pink as blood, I think of Dante and Virgil clambering down Satan's hairy flanks at the bottom of the Inferno, grabbing fistfuls of his thick, dark pelt as they ladder their way out, into the other, brighter hemisphere.

Though Sam is a good dog, and gentle, and soft. It wasn't

his fault that he flushed out a skunk and chased it back into the woods. He was acting on instinct, like any dog. He stopped, stiffened, then shot off, baying, not thinking about the consequences—that rank, acrid, stinging cloud, smoky somehow, like burning rubber. A golden retriever doesn't make decisions. It doesn't reason.

And I squeeze out the ketchup on his shoulders, his neck, his tail, smearing in the clots and streaks, and the sweetness rises, the thick, sweet smell, cloying against the foulness and the stink.

The Latin root of the word "monster" is *monstrum*, as in *monstrance*, the receptacle in which the consecrated host is displayed, the very Body of Christ. It means *show*.

As a noun: *Sign. Portent.*

The dark woods and the morning stars. The driveway running pink. And I scrub and I hose, sluicing, spraying, the force of the water fanning back the golden fur.

Underneath, the pale, white skin.

We are made in the image and likeness of God, and deep down underneath the layers isn't something ugly and unlovable and vile but something beautiful and precious and beyond price. The sin in the Garden wasn't that we were naked but that we were ashamed to be.

"If God loves me," someone once told me, "he can love anybody."

I know she was joking and I know what she means, but there's an assumption underneath this all the same, an assumption I think most of us make, and it's wrong. Jesus loves us not in spite of who we are but because of it—because we are lovely, and ordinary, and precious, and good.

Jesus forgives us, as he forgives Peter. He is always forgiving us; he will never stop forgiving us. He is never shocked or put off or discouraged with us.

In a way he isn't calling us to change. He is calling us to be ourselves, truly ourselves—to let go of the masks and disguises.

It's not just that Jesus is our beloved friend. It's that we are his, and we deny him when we deny this.

CHAPTER 6

Laughing at Ourselves

You know how when you're running late and it's raining and you can't find a parking place, you can't find one anywhere, you're going crazy, and instinctively you pray, O God, help me find a parking place!

Michael Casey says that in a way this is exactly right, because in moments like this we're forced to admit again what he calls our "inner incompetence"—how really we're still children, lost and lonely and in need of help.

Sometimes we can't figure out the simplest things, we can't get through a normal day—everything defeats us—and unless we admit this to ourselves and to God, unless we step back and laugh at ourselves, we'll never grow in our faith.

Once in high school I was driving to the lake, my Chevy full of seniors, all of us laughing and talking. I was gesturing and waving my arms, talking intently, trying to make a point, when a state patrolman turned on his lights and pulled me over. He'd been tailing me for several minutes. He got out of his cruiser, walked to my window, and leaned in, a tall, stern man in a Smokey Bear hat.

"I have to write you a ticket," he said, drawling, "for failing to pay attention."

I was mad in Jerusalem on the Via Dolorosa, because Barb had missed the bus and the little tractors that pulled the garbage wagons kept shuddering and clattering and the hawkers hawked and the pilgrims clumped and the Muslims in the Muslim Quarter who see this every day were seeing it again.

In the evening, during Holy Hour, back at the Church of All Nations at Gethsemane, it was resentment welling up in me, and I thought how ludicrous the church is and how on earth can it stand? My back hurt. It was night. The roar of traffic on the freeway outside, especially trucks.

There was that moment, too, on the Mount of Beatitudes when I looked out at the Sea of Galilee, at the shining gray waters, and I felt something like joy welling up in me and a sense of the presence of something gathering me in. The fields and groves.

Late afternoon in the Valley of Doves.

The guides kept telling us Jesus walked here or Jesus broiled fish there or Jesus stood in the boat and shouted here, in this cove, his voice carrying over the waters, bringing us solace and hope, but all I kept thinking that was whatever particular rock he sat on, or wherever his feet may or may not have trod, when I looked out at the water and the mountains and trees, or at the yearning of the people in their hope and their need, or when I looked within, at myself, I at least was seeing what he saw.

———

The funny thing about sin is that it's no big deal. Not when we pay attention.

The funny thing is that when we get practiced at seeing

and naming our faults, early and often, they shrink. They become ordinary—persistent but manageable.

"How great a forest is set ablaze by a small fire," James says, talking about sins of the tongue, gossiping, getting angry. It's easy to dismiss sins like this and explain them away because only words are involved, only language. But James's point is that little things can make a difference.

And this is the source of the joy, of the liberation, because there's something I can do. I need grace—I need the grace of God in all things—but I can certainly stop swearing at the dog. I can say no to a second piece of pie. Even the Seven Deadly Sins in the Catholic tradition—Pride, Envy, Anger, Avarice, Sloth, Gluttony, and Lust—are clear and straightforward, and that clarity can help us spot them early, before they get too big and hard to control.

It's like untying a knot. It's like getting an MRI: our vague, pervasive sense of feeling lousy gets clarified. It's a disc, a clear, fixable thing.

The problem isn't God! It's me! Isn't that great?

It's not that God doesn't exist, but that I don't. Not fully.

I clean off my glasses. I feel my small gears engaging the great gears, coming into alignment with the great pattern.

The Babylonians have destroyed the temple in Jerusalem, they have sent the leaders of Israel into exile, and the psalmist cries out, in his grief and his rage, in the shocking last lines of Psalm 137: "O daughter Babylon, you devastator! / Happy shall they be who pay you back / what you have done to us! / Happy shall they be who take your little ones / and dash them against the rock!"

Violence. Vengeance.

But we don't have to read these lines literally. We can do what the early Church Fathers do and internalize them, seeing "the enemy" as a symbol of our evil desires, of our sinfulness, and particularly, in this psalm, of how small our sins are in the beginning, and weak, and easy to track. C. S. Lewis even turns his interpretation of Psalm 137 into a joke—a serious joke, a joke on us—reading the babies as "the infantile beginnings" of "small indulgences" and "small resentments" that "woo us and wheedle us" and seem "so tiny, so helpless."

"Against all such pretty infants," Lewis concludes, "the advice of the Psalm is best. Knock the little bastards' brains out."

This is the attitude: direct and matter-of-fact.

———

The guide hurries us past the *Pieta*, Michelangelo's glorious statue, early one morning in Rome. We just glimpse it, to the right, in the high, dim air of St. Peter's, empty for a moment more, before the crowds flood in—a flash of the luminous marble limbs, still in shadow. The crucified body of our Lord, limp in his mother's lap.

The pews are marble, too, white marble, and the ambo and the floors below in the crypt, in the Chapel of the Tomb of Saint Peter, where I stand and preach to our own little busload, in their jeans and walking shoes, nametags dangling. Connie and Al and Diane. Janet and Jim. My balding baby brother, middle-aged now, like me.

And at first I think, I shouldn't be preaching at St. Peter's. I shouldn't be here.

But then I realize: Who better? Like Peter, I jump out of the boat and sink a hundred times a day.

The struggle never ends, even as we advance in the spiritual life. Even a life of prayer and mass and spiritual reading and good works, even a good, faithful life doesn't make the darkness go away. In fact, as we progress, things get worse. We become more aware. In the Buddhist tradition, as Pema Chodron explains, this is called "heightened neurosis." Even on our deathbed, she says, we'll be irritated about something: the nurse, the pillow, the light coming through the window.

"We never graduate from a state of being utterly dependent on God's mercy and forgiveness," Casey says. "The shadow is part of our reality, and so in a spirit of faith, we thank God also for the darkness in our life."

This is what the *examen* is for: to help us become skilled in seeing and accepting ourselves. Every day we look back on the moments, checking in with the fifth chapter of Galatians, with its listing of "the fruits of the Spirit" and "the fruits of the flesh," and checking off which set of feelings is at work in us—wrangling and jealousy or patience and kindness and peace. Every day we keep track of the light and keep track of the darkness.

And not in a "woe-is-me-I'm-so-terrible" sense but in the sense of laughing at ourselves and moving on, in the sense of saying, Of course, what did I expect? Thank you, Jesus. I trust in you, Jesus. You're the one who can heal me, and I will be healed.

O God, I know you love me for who I really am, this person running late, in the rain, who can't find a parking place.

Pema Chodron recommends three things:

First, we need to simply acknowledge when we've been triggered. Caught up. Hooked. Admit it. Learn the signs: the tightening in the neck, the balling of the fists.

Second, we need to pause, take three conscious breaths, and simply "abide" with the feeling. Stay with it. Not act on it, but not judge it, either. Not try to repress it. Let it happen.

Third, we need to relax and move on. The feeling will pass, if we let it. It will always pass.

Not that even these small steps are easy, of course. We're hooked so often and at such deep levels that we're lucky if we can become aware of it even once or twice a day. But even that small awareness would make an enormous difference, not just in our own lives but in the lives of others. It would change the world.

Even years into her ministry for the poor, Dorothy Day, the founder of the Catholic Worker Movement, was making mistakes and feeling anger and frustration—and admitting it, and asking for forgiveness:

I need to overcome a sense of my own impotence, my own failure, and an impatience at others that goes with it. Such a sense of defeat comes from expecting too much of one's self, also from a sense of pride. More and more I realize how good God is to me to send me discouragements, failures, antagonisms. The only way to proceed is to remember that God's ways are not our ways. To bear our own burdens, to do our own work as best we can, and not fret because we cannot do more or do another's work.

We're always being triggered, and we always will be. We're always being hooked. Someone says something about the church or the president or someone in our families, and instantly we're mad, we're upset, without even thinking about it, really.

We never get better. We just get better at not getting better.

———

When Dorothy Day died in 1980, at the age of eighty-three, they found in her final diary a prayer card with this fifth-century prayer from St. Ephrem:

O Lord and master of my life, take from me the spirit of sloth, faintheartedness, lust of power and idle talk. But give to thy servant rather the spirit of chastity, humility, patience, and love. Yea, O Lord and King, grant me to see my own errors and not to judge my brother, for thou art blessed from all ages to ages.

———

A dissection class.

Who could have guessed the cadaver would be someone she had known years before, a beloved teacher, with his grizzled beard and thinning hair, or how beautiful he would be when they flipped him over and slit him open and the ganglion of nerves at the base of his spine spilled out into the air, the *cauda equina,* a gathering of filaments for a moment so luminous, so like pearl, all the students wept behind their masks?

"Lord," Pope Francis prays, in *The Joy of the Gospel,* "I have let myself be deceived; in a thousand ways I have shunned your love, yet here I am once more, to renew my covenant with you. I need you. Save me once again, Lord, take me once more into your redeeming embrace."

When I see my friend Marty and I ask him what he's been doing, he says he's been working on the Mars mission. The Mars mission!

Marty's an oceanographer, and the rover is crawling now, inch by inch, with its googly camera eyes and spindly tractor wheels, over the dry floor of an ancient sea millions of miles away, and Marty sits before a screen and watches the graphs appear and the pictures come in, pixel by pixel, and he studies every granule, every speck, molecule by molecule, and he doesn't care how long it takes—it could take months to travel across your own front porch at this rate, months to examine the light and the texture of the first thing you happen to look at when you wake up in the morning, the threads in your sheets, the angle of the sun—because this is how it should be, this slow, careful seeing, this painstaking study, entirely without judgment, entirely without prejudice or hope, even if you never find signs of life, no spark at all, only rock and sand and the ordinary granules and the wind like any other wind since time immemorial and even before, neither life nor death nor fear nor hope.

How Marty's face lights up as he tells me. That reality is so lovely.

Walter Burghardt's definition of prayer: "a long, loving look at the real."

He also says, "The real I look at. I do not analyze or argue it, describe or define it. . . . I do not move around it: I enter into it."

———

Imagine the perfect church. All the doctrines you agree with. Every structure just.

You'd still have to wake up in the morning. You'd still have to look at yourself in the mirror.

Anthony de Mello's advice: Whenever you're mad at somebody else or upset about a group of people or a large, abstract issue, really worked up, look inside. There's something in you that you don't want to face. What is it?

———

And then we laugh it off, in a good way—the darkness, our limitations. It's not awful and depressing to face reality. We just stand back and see it. We say, Oh, here this feeling is again. This is happening again. We don't give in to the feeling, but we don't fight it, either. We acknowledge it. We see the moment as simply part of the fabric of life, part of the ebb and flow.

It's raining and I'm late and I can't find a parking place, and I step back and see myself in the rain and see myself late and anxious and suddenly, for a moment, I'm free. I laugh. Of course. Then, whether I find a parking place or not, it's good, it's all good, as people are always saying, but it is, because I realize none of this is important. Whether I find a parking place or not, I'm still me and I'm still loved by God and God doesn't love me any less because I'm stressed out and frustrated—and God will never love me any less. And I'm not a hero. I'm no different from anyone else. However much I've prayed the rosary or worked at Stone Soup or done the things I try to do, I'm still a child, I'm still a person.

That's when Jesus heals us: when we let him.

Hitchhiking from Scotland when I was nineteen. Bare yellow hills. Pale blue sky. I was trying to have an adventure, but all I did was wait. Once I got a ride with an old woman and her pug—once with a refrigerator salesman, all the way to Carlisle. But then another scrubby interchange. The wind bending the grasses.

That night I finally knocked on the door of a lorry parked on the side of the motorway, and the driver let me sleep in back, shivering in the faux leather jacket I'd bought in Spokane with some of the money I made working at Safeway all summer, stocking shelves and imagining myself in England.

In the morning, squeezed between the driver and his mate on the way to Stoke-on-Trent, I had to pee so badly my eyes began to water. Long gray factories. Warehouse after warehouse.

We spend all our lives trying to find ourselves. And we do.

Angel! Angel! I hear a woman crying deep in the woods one morning. She is calling for her dog, a squat, white cattle dog, pot-bellied, bowlegged—I've seen it, I tell her, trotting along the trail.

One ear flat. Tongue dragging. Just as happy as could be.

Someone parked behind me in the Beanery parking lot and I'm trapped, I can't back out, but there's a space to the left, and I think maybe I can angle and scooch my way clear.

And as I start a man comes out to get into his truck and stops to help me. "You've been screwed," he says, and steps to where I can see him in my rearview mirror, and waves with his hands and measures the air with his hands and holds his hands up to stop me as I crank the wheel and ease forward, then straighten the wheel and ease back, forward and back, forward and back, sidling, sidling, until in the end another man comes out, and the man who's been helping me calls him over to measure and shout from the front, too, as slowly, slowly, I get within inches of clearing.

The new man has a beard. The first man, in back, is stubbly and thin and wears a black leather jacket. Is smiling. Is a Good Samaritan.

The key thing is to listen. To inch forward.

The key thing is not to think. Trust. Again, and again, and again.

CHAPTER 7

Learning to Serve

I'm watching Carson in his stiff white collar serving cana-pés in the library at Downton Abbey, and something about it seems familiar. He leans over and holds out a silver tray, then quietly steps back. Lord and Lady Grantham, and Lady Mary, and the Dowager Duchess, and all the others, chatting and drinking tea in that great, wood-paneled room. A gray light coming through the high windows.

And then it hits me. Of course—being a deacon is like this. Spreading the corporal on the altar to prepare for communion. Arranging the shining bowls and cups. Pouring the wine. I'm wearing a white robe with a high collar. I keep handing things to the priest—the silver patent, the silver chalice—then quietly stepping back, just off his right shoulder. The congregation waits in the pews, beneath the great, high ceilings of the church.

The Greek word *diakonia*, "servant," is one of the words most often used to describe Jesus in the Gospels: Jesus, who is always listening and healing and washing the feet of others.

We are all called to be servants, to be deacons, and we

are all ambivalent about it. It's a great honor, and it's demeaning, too. On the one hand, we don't want to play second banana, always in the background; on the other hand, we feel too selfish to be called deacons, not good enough to claim to be like Jesus in any way.

In the language of the church, an ordained deacon serving on the altar and in the world is a "sacramental sign" of Christ the servant—a visible representation of what we are all called to be. But the deacon is also a sacramental sign of our uneasiness about this. Our reluctance and our joy. Our resistance and our satisfaction.

Once I got a call from a funeral home in Albany asking me to bless a body before cremation. The family didn't want a service, but they did want something. So I put on my collar, picked up my alb and stole, and drove through the June fields and over the bridge.

The funeral home was in an old building covered with ivy. Flies buzzed at the entrance. Inside it was all faded velvet and overstuffed furniture and heavy, tasseled drapes, and there, around a corner, on a fabric-draped bier, was the body, covered from the waist down with the kind of tattered quilt a grandmother might make. Brown hair combed back. Brown goatee, going to gray. The man had been a roofer and was wearing a blue t-shirt with the name of his roofing company on it, and in his hand he was holding a remote—a remote for a satellite TV.

I was surprised by the remote, but it didn't bother me, really. I have one exactly like it. Beige, with black buttons. The man was my age. I think I even recognized him, though I don't know from where.

The name of the funeral home director was Wally. He was about our age, too, and it was just the three of us—Wally, the dead man, and me. Behind us, in a horseshoe, a dozen velvet chairs. An empty room. Heavy drapes. I didn't put on my vestments. I just opened my book and read the prayers in a loud voice, then traced the sign of the cross in the air above the body, and I was glad to do it: *Eternal rest grant unto him, O Lord. / And let perpetual light shine upon him.* It wasn't right in a way, to give the blessing without the family there, but it felt right. As I was saying the words, I had the sense of performing a small, useful task.

Michael Mayberry. That was the name of the man with the remote.

Michael Mayberry.

"The deacon is one who waits," Mark Santer says. "He is never in charge. He is the servant of others—of God, of his bishop, of the congregation. He is a voice. It is his task to read the Lord's Gospel, not his own. He is a servant: it is his task to wait at the Lord's table. . . . It is others who preside; he is the waiter, the attendant."

Deacons have "faculties" to baptize, to witness weddings, and to do memorial services—in that sense deacons preside—and they have the opportunity to preach now and then. But a deacon can't say mass, and the baptisms and weddings and memorials where deacons preside are shorter and stand alone, without the Eucharist. Usually a deacon is called when the family isn't Catholic or isn't practicing, or there's a Catholic marrying a non-Catholic, or a priest can't be found. Into these borders. These margins.

Only a priest can do what Catholics call the anointing of the sick, but I decided to buy some essential oil from a health food store, concentrated scent of rose, and put a little on the palms of my friend, Dorinda, who was dying. It was very strong. It filled the room. At first I thought I'd made a mistake. I thought, I'll never get it off my hands and my clothes.

But back at school, as I answered my emails and taught my classes, I realized: she was with me. I was carrying her with me.

And white swans in a green field on the way back from the nursing home.

And spring. Misty rain. Daffodils and tulips.

"Is there anything at all that is peculiar to a deacon?" Santer asks. "Is he given powers that are given to no one else? The answer is 'No' ... But that is just what is distinctive about him. He has no power, he is a servant."

That same day I put a whole, round host on Dorinda's soft, parched tongue, and she started choking and thrashing around. People who are dying have dry mouths, and they're lying down, their heads on pillows. I had to give Dorinda three sips of water before she could swallow, lifting her from her shoulders, head forward, chin on her chest.

That would be bad, I said, to choke to death on the Body of Christ, and she started coughing again, weakly, she started to laugh, and I did, too.

Who do you think you are? the old man shouted, stumbling up the aisle with his little dog, a shaggy, long-haired dachshund, coppery red. *Who do you think you are?* in his tattered sweater and dirty blue Mariners cap. Waving his arms.

I was preaching the gospel. I was standing at the ambo in my alb and my stole proclaiming the love of God. The people in the pews. Soon the Body of Christ.

So I stepped down and met him, at the foot of the altar, taking him by the elbow and turning him around. *You are welcome*, I said, whispering in his ear. *You are welcome.*

For I knew him. I knew who he was.

———

I don't know all that the cross of Christ means, but I do know it makes psychological sense. Sooner or later we have to face the suffering and emptiness and apparent randomness of the world and of our powerlessness before it. And until then, we can't be healthy. That's the paradox. Until we admit our need, we can never be happy.

And that's what Christ did. He embraced the emptiness, so completely and lovingly he transformed it forever. As Dermot Lane puts it:

> *The paradox at the heart of Christianity is about the isolated ego becoming a relational being, the indifferent self becoming an active subject in solidarity with others, the lonely individual discovering his or her real center of gravity in others and in God.*

To follow the path of Christ is to follow the steps of the therapeutic process. To be a Christian is to be psychologically whole. Whatever else it is, the story of Jesus is the story of the letting go and the giving up we have to do every day of our lives.

And there's the joy. In exactly the second we realize this, at exactly the moment of letting go, a light comes flooding in. Jesus did not deem equality with God "something to be exploited" but rather "emptied himself" and became a servant, even a "slave." And "therefore"—this key turn, this logical consequence—"he is highly exalted," and to him "every knee must bend."

We have to die to our false selves to rise to the new.

To be a deacon is to be put into situations where again and again we have to act out this dying whether we want to or not. Again and again we are given chances to die and chances to realize how we don't want to.

To look at a deacon serving on the altar is to be reminded of our own lives: this uselessness, this struggle, this playfulness, this joy.

In the observation car, while the ocean and sky and the edge of the land with its rocks and trees keep flowing behind her, my friend listens to three young hipsters drinking wine and laughing and making jokes about Jesus. Short hair and skinny jeans. Horn-rimmed glasses.

Making fun of the Lord.

When a flock of pelicans catches up to the window, matching the speed of the train.

Six brown pelicans seeming to hang for a moment, suspended in the air outside, in silhouette, a few feet away, with their improbable bills and their great flapping wings, their ugly feet tucked up in the feathers of their bellies.

And everyone turns to look and exclaim; everything is suspended.

And she thought, O Lord, I love these three young men. O Lord, I love you, in whom we live and move and have our being.

There comes a point when we realize we're no big deal after all, and neither is anyone else, and that's OK. That's all there is—these small acts, these moments—and there's something endearing about that, and homely, and sweet.

The Lord of all the universe become a particular person in a particular body.

"We all have to discover," Jean Vanier says, "there are others like us who have gifts and needs; no one of us is the center of the world. We are a small but important part of our universe. We all have a part to play. We need one another."

And there's this sense of lightness, and freedom, and relief.

All we have to do is what we have to do.

Here. Now.

It is "one adorable point of the incredible condescension of the Incarnation," as Gerard Manley Hopkins puts it, that the creator of the universe should "consent to be taught carpentering."

Jesus "thought it no snatching-matter for him to be equal with God but annihilated himself," taking the form of a slave, and it is "this holding himself back, and not snatching at the truest and highest good," that is the root of his holiness, and "the imitation of this the root of all moral good in others."

When Maggie was three days old, we brought her home from the hospital. I walked back into the living room, and there she was on the couch, still swaddled in the hospital blanket, and she was so perfect and so beautiful that I walked over and kneeled. I kneeled because I wanted to be close to her, to put my face next to hers, and that's why we kneel in church.

Christ is all our daughters and all our sons. Christ is everything beautiful and perfect, and she's sleeping on the couch. He is lying in the manger. All we should want is to be close to him. All we should ever want is to kneel and put our face next to his.

We are all of us deacons. There is something greater and more important and more beautiful than who we are alone. There is the body; there is sadness; there is death. There are other people, and history, and tradition—all these things we didn't create. There is joy beyond measure.

I drive up to Hillsboro to St. Matthew's to do a wedding for a student.

I'm such a pro. I know what I'm doing.

The problem is that the ambo at St. Matthew's is elevated—you have to walk up two steps—and when I went to proclaim the gospel, I forgot about this. There I was, standing in front of several hundred people, and when I turned around, not thinking, I fell off the steps. I had to grab the edge of the ambo to keep from hitting my chin, and even then I was looking up, at my feet, in the air. It's a miracle I didn't hurt myself.

I got up and the wedding went on. Everything happened anyway.

Driving home, I started to laugh. Up the mountain and down into the valley. I kept thinking of our silly pretentions, our false pride. I kept thinking how beautiful the world was, the winter trees and the sky. I kept thinking how I'd look on *America's Funniest Home Videos*: there one second, gone the next.

Maybe in a way that's my vocation, and yours, too: to fall and to keep falling.

———

Teilhard de Chardin says this about death:

God must in some way or other make room for Himself, hollowing us out and emptying us, if He is finally to penetrate into us. And in order to assimilate us in Him, he must break the molecules of our being so as to recast and re-model us. The function of death is to provide the necessary entrance into our inmost selves. It will make us undergo the required disassociation. It will put us into the state organically needed if the fire is to descend upon us. And in that way its fatal power to decompose and dissolve will be harnessed to the most sublime operations of life. What was by nature empty and void can, in each human existence, become plenitude and unity in God.

This is the function of the diaconate for the deacon: to provide the necessary entrance into our inmost selves. This is what the diaconate reminds us all of: the required disassociation.

De Mello asks us to think of a child who is given a taste for drugs and becomes addicted. He says that this is what our culture does to us when we are born. We are given a taste for "the drug called approval, appreciation, attention."

But not Jesus. The Pharisees in Matthew are right about one thing, when they dispute with him about the census tax and what is owed to Caesar: Jesus "isn't concerned with anyone's opinion." He says to render unto Caesar what is Caesar's, and to render unto God what is God's, and he knows nothing he says will convince them, and he doesn't care. He's not trying to look good.

But we do care, and we are trying to look good. Often that's our real motive when we get into arguments about faith—not to help the other person but to convince that person and the world and maybe most of all ourselves that we're as smart and cool as anyone else. We want to win the argument so we can win approval.

In one of his "Sabbath" poems Wendell Berry talks about "the politics of illusion, of death's money," and how these possess us. These illusions, he says, are hell. And then, alluding to the Gospel of John, Berry goes on to describe how Jesus rose from the politics and rose from the money and strode "godly forth": so free of fear and so free of shame he appears to Mary Magdalene to be "only the gardener, walking about in the new day, among the flowers."

"Death's money" makes me think of the coin Jesus uses in his argument with the Pharisees; "the politics of illusion," how we get caught up in the wrong arguments and care about the wrong things. But more important is the image of how Jesus when he rises is so free of those fantasies and so free of those false values that other people, even his beloved Mary, mistake him for the gardener.

It's early spring, and I want to burn my burn pile. Branches and leaves. Parts of a fence. But the recycling has already come, and there isn't any newspaper. So I decide to use old drafts of poems.

As I slip the pages into the hollows of the tangled pile, I keep glancing at old stanzas and lines.

But the fire won't build. It flares, then dies, first one corner, then another, the twigs and leaves catching fire but not the soggy branches, until I've fed it every sheet I have, and all that's left are ashes. Not even a hundred abandoned drafts of poems can produce the necessary heat.

Only smoke—the sweet, leafy smoke of spring— a soft, gray plume, rising above the cherry trees. A wreath.

Let my prayer be counted as incense before you;
and the lifting up of my hands as an evening sacrifice.

At the end of mass I stand by the credence table, purifying the cups after communion. Everyone else is on their knees, waiting until the priest finishes his tasks on the altar and sits back down in the presider's chair. Then the soft rumble of the congregation getting up and sitting down, too.

But I stand to the side, by the tabernacle, pouring water into one cup and swishing it around, pouring the water from that cup into the next and swishing it around, until I get to the last cup, the one I will drink.

And there, in the bottom of the final cup, I see what I think is a piece of the host floating in the water. Something white. Shimmering. A piece of the Body of Christ.

But it's not. It's my own reflection, mirrored in the water, upside down, like in an old-fashioned camera. My own white hair. My own pale face. The surface of the water rippling for a moment, like a pond in the wind.

Until I lift the cup and drink. I drink it all in.

"Give joy to your servant, Lord," cries the Psalmist, "for to you I lift up my soul."

It is good "to sing praises to your name, O Most High," says another psalm, "to the music of the lute and the harp, to the melody of the lyre."

"At the works of your hands I sing for joy."

A ukulele band strums by the grave of an old woman I never knew. I lead the prayers, alb flapping, helping to lay the body to rest, and as the family lingers, I quietly walk away, down the hill to another grave I remember from before.

It was winter then and the oak was bare and the one we buried was a boy. "I keep thinking he'll be cold," the father said. "He'll need his coat."

But it's summer now, and the farmers are haying in their yellow fields. The dust of the harvest is softening the air. And as I stand at the marker looking out, a kind of peace comes over me, almost like the peace we prayed for up the hill, the peace of God, which surpasses all understanding. It spreads through my body like warmth.

I know. I'm just saying what happened. I'm just saying that it surprised me, too. The farmers, and the yellow fields, and the warm summer wind.

The ukulele band, strumming still.

We don't want to be mistaken for the gardener. We don't want to be seen as simple and plain. We want to be seen as smart. We want to win the arguments. But we're not going to win, and it's not going to matter anyway. We're going to be crucified, we're going to be underestimated, but we're also going to rise, we're going to be free, and the garden we'll be walking in then will be the Garden of Eden, it will be the earthly paradise, our glimpse, our foretaste, of heaven.

PART III

SEEING GOD IN EVERYTHING

Remember that these things are mysteries,
and that if they were such that you could understand them,
they wouldn't be worth understanding.
A God you understood would be less than yourself.

—Flannery O'Connor

CHAPTER 8

Going Wild

He saw it crumpled on the side of the road and thought at first it was a dog. But when he stopped and took a closer look, he saw the tufted ears and the broad, flat nose, the dusty, spotted fur, and he knew it was a bobcat, and he knew it wasn't dead. It was battered and bloody, but it wasn't dead; it was breathing, the flanks heaving up and down.

So he got to his knees, and he took the bobcat in his arms—it was smaller than he thought it would be, and lighter—it was panting, and rank, and warm—and he gently laid it on the backseat of his car. Wrapping it in a towel, maybe. Putting his hands, for a moment, in the dusty fur.

Then he slipped behind the wheel and drove—to where? A clinic? A shelter? I'm not sure—I don't know what was in his mind—and I don't remember what happened next, as he was driving, when he looked into his mirror and saw the bobcat beginning to stir, opening one yellow eye, flexing one velvet paw, whether he stepped on the accelerator and drove faster, or pulled over again and opened the back door and crouched behind it, waiting for the bobcat to slink away.

I don't remember now how the story ended, and I don't think it matters.

A bobcat lay on the side of the road, battered and panting and warm, and it was splendid. It was wild.

And he stopped. He knelt before it. He took it in his arms.

We have to act. We have to discern what we think God wants us to do tomorrow. Should we say yes or should we say no?

But we can only act in the moment and for the moment, in the face of the questions and in the midst of the questions. What we kneel before is splendid and it is wild and we have to take it in our arms.

My Lord God, Thomas Merton prays, "I have no idea where I am going. I do not see the road ahead of me. I cannot know for certain where it will end." But somehow, he believes, God will lead him, though he "may know nothing about it." He will trust in him, though he "may seem to be lost and in the shadow of death."

When I lived for a month in the hut by the sea, back home my little red dog ran away. I was walking in the alder, on the point above the bay, and the thought crossed my mind: Lucy has run away. And she had, I found out, that day, and she didn't come back for hours.

It wasn't an intuition, exactly. It was just a thought.

But all those thirty days I was more porous than usual, more aware of the signs that God sends us, or might, and I often missed Lucy and thought about her. I kept seeing her face in the faces of the deer and the chipmunks and even the birds. I became aware that everything has a face. We have eyes and so do the animals. We have ears and so do they. They kept me company in that lonely month when I was trying to pray and sometimes feeling thinned out, opened. Sunsets. Clouds coming and going. Dreams. Once, touching the trunk of the tree.

Since then I've suffered several losses, and it's been harder to stay on the path and follow the call than I thought it would be. Sometimes where we find ourselves is in the desert. More and more, I think, life is about letting things go, or trying to. It's about giving things up. It's about holding things in memory and believing in them still.

The night before I gave Lucy away, I brushed her long red hair until it shone, combing out the tangles. She leaned against me as I worked, and I hugged her and talked to her. "Oh, Lucy," I whispered. "I have to."

In the morning, when she hopped into his car and my friend drove her away, she looked from the back like a beautiful young girl.

Now a metal gate has clanged down on the road where I walked, blocking the way. The sanctuary is closed.

Sold to help settle another abuse case.

And now the buildings have been burned down. The Neskowin Volunteer Fire Department has used the lodge for practice, and the hut and the cabins—they set them all aflame, and the walls burned and the ceilings burned and I guess all that remains is what always remains: the sky and the sea and the earth itself.

Our eyes are burning and all that they see. Our ears are burning and all that they hear.

My theophany.

(*Theophany: theo + phany*: an experience of God)

I'd been fasting and praying, I'd been studying the Bible, and God appeared before me, clear as day, in a white robe and with a flowing beard, and in a deep, resonant voice he said to me, My son, because you are so morally pure and spiritually advanced, I have chosen to explain to you the secret of life. And he did. Everything was clear. I understood everything then, and I still do. The Big Bang. Why people suffer.

At the end God handed me a plastic card the size of a credit card, and with it I can judge the moral worth of the people I see—whether they're good enough or not. And if you doubt me, I can show you the card, not to mention the video I took with my smartphone. I've got proof.

I was so calm while this was going on, so happy, and I have been ever since. People love me. Money pours in. I go from triumph to triumph, utterly confident, utterly serene.

Which of course is nothing like the theophanies in the Bible, the theophanies of Abraham and his family in Genesis or of anyone else from the Old Testament to the New.

Genesis doesn't tell us anything about Abraham at first. We don't know why he was chosen, he just was, and we don't know what God looks like or sounds like or anything about him except that he comes. "The Lord said to Abram, 'Go from your country.'" That's all. The language of Genesis is wonderfully minimal, and that spareness speaks volumes. It tells us that God is beyond language, beyond understanding.

In the theophanies later in Genesis, Abraham is taken

out to see the vastness of the stars, or he is sleeping, or in a kind of trance—these experiences almost always take place at night or in the threshold times. And far from understanding everything clearly, Abraham later laughs out loud, he falls on his face and laughs, as Sarah laughs, too, bitterly, because what God promises is so improbable: Me, an old man, become the father of the nations? Me, a barren old woman, a mother after all these years?

From the minute Abraham receives the call, his life gets more complicated than it was before. He wanders over the desert; he has to battle other tribes; he has to deal with family squabbles and tensions. A son is finally born, and Sarah laughs in joy, and they name their son Isaac, which means "laughter," but when the child is older, God asks Abraham to take him out and offer him as a human sacrifice, only staying the knife at the last minute.

Down the generations, through Jacob and Joseph and the twelve tribes, this is one big, dysfunctional family, torn apart by violence and hatred and sexual abuse.

I fall asleep feeling heavy and sad. I know my faith should be stronger, I know I should have more trust, but this feeling has gotten into me, this heaviness: we are born and then we die. We disappear.

A warm spring night, the anniversary of my mother's death. Sweet air pours through the open window.

Midnight I am awakened by deer. They mince through the dry winter leaves beneath the trees, two, three of them, right up to the house. Inches away. As they approach, they make a sound like crumpling paper. Then the tearing of the grass as they feed. The dry rasping of their ruminations. Only the sheetrock separates us, and the screens.

Finally, grumbling, I jump up, throw on my robe and slippers, and run out the door, shouting as I round the corner, never seeing, only sensing, the dark, animal weight of their bodies before they go pounding away, crashing through the branches.

For a moment I stand in the yard. The dewy grass. The cool air. The jagged trees.

And the stars. All above me, the stars. The brilliant, unimaginable stars.

―――――――

"If we wish to see and hear a person's soul," Parker Palmer says, "there is a truth we must remember":

The soul is like a wild animal—tough, resilient, and yet shy. When we go crashing through the woods shouting for it to come out so we can help it, the soul will stay in hiding. But if we are willing to sit quietly and wait a while, the soul may show itself.

―――――――

Where are you? This is God's question to Adam and Eve in the Garden, after they've sinned. *What is this that you have done?* Good questions.

The questions at the heart of the *examen*.

Am I my brother's keeper? This is Cain's question after he murders Abel, and it's a good one, too. Am I responsible for others, and how?

Who am I? Moses asks before the burning bush, in the wilderness. Who am I to do such an enormous thing? What is my nature? What is my identity?

There are questions all over the Bible, they're everywhere, and what if we focused on *them* for a while? What if that's the point of the Bible: not to settle things but to open them up. What if that's what the church really is: people living together with the questions.

Jesus is more a teller of stories and an asker of questions than anything else. "Why are you grumbling?" "Which man did the right thing?" "Who do you say that I am?" The Gospels are a tissue of questions, and not just the questions *of* Jesus but the questions *about* him, including the wrong questions, the stupid ones, as in the Gospel of John, with the Samaritan woman at the well. When Jesus says he brings "a living water," the Samaritan woman takes him literally. The Samaritan woman again—our representative, our stand-in. Where is this water? she asks the Lord. Does that mean I don't have to keep using the well? When Jesus tells the disciples he has spiritual food, in this same scene, they turn to one another: Did someone get him a sandwich? Has he eaten already? This is how it is. We live on the surface; we ask the wrong questions. How can we impress our boss? How long will it take us to firm up our abs?

No, Jesus says. His whole ministry is one long, difficult effort to get us to change the questions we ask, to learn the compassion and humility we need to live without the black-and-white rules of the Pharisees and the others. He doesn't often succeed—look at what happens to him in the end—but in the case of the woman at the well, he does, through patient listening, through a long, sustained conversation. Finally she gets beyond the literal and the flat and the closed. Finally she knows who Jesus is, and she knows because she's experienced him, in the flesh, in his person.

In a way the woman's first question is more profound than she realizes. *Where can I get this living water?* Yes. That's the only question worth asking.

Look at the disciples in the Gospel. Peter is the rock on which the church is built, and he's the one who denies Jesus three times. In the Transfiguration scene he's so overwhelmed he makes a complete fool of himself, wanting to build booths and pin things down that can't be pinned down, and a few passages later he's arguing with the other disciples about who will be first in the kingdom. The disciples have no idea what's going on. They don't get it. They keep being stubborn, flawed human beings even after they're chosen, and even as disciples, even as friends of Jesus, they have to suffer and struggle the rest of their lives.

And this is good news, it really is, because it means that when we are confused and when we deny Jesus and when we suffer, we can see this confusion and failure and suffering as sacred, as part of the journey, as leading to the Promised Land. When we turn out to be human like everyone else, we can see our frailty as continued proof of our need for grace, and we can be grateful, because that grace always comes, is always pouring down on us.

We can laugh in disbelief, we can laugh in bitterness,

we can laugh in joy, for all our laughter is blessed, all our laughter is true. Everything is theophany.

———————

It's a forest, Cardinal Newman says: Scripture is a forest, "unsystematic and various." It cannot be mapped; it must remain "an unexplored and unsubdued land."

———————

Pericope means "to cut away" in Greek. It's the term for the short passages the Bible is made of, because that's what the Bible is: a mosaic, a stitching together of pericopes, the language spare and brief and stark. The Bible is stories and sayings and teachings and stunned, joyous, eye-witness accounts—all from different sources, from different times and places, but brought together and *redacted*—another good word to know, as in "edited"—redacted into the text we have now, the collage we have now, from Genesis to Revelation. The Bible is a blended and woven and orchestrated series of fragments and pieces, but with gaps, too, big gaps in between, big jumps sometimes, and these are important, too, just as important, because it's here, in the spaces, in the silences, we hear God speak.

I think of a shop in the Armenian Quarter in Jerusalem, of these fine painted tiles and lovely little pots, and, above the shelves, a painting of the ancient wall and the towers and the Dome of the Rock spread across several large terracotta tiles.

But the tiles have been broken into dozens of pieces, they've been shattered, deliberately, and the fragments put back together at angles, their jagged edges showing.

The artist is sitting behind the counter. He says, *That's the real Jerusalem.*

"I have become like a broken vessel," says Psalm 31.

———

There is a plan, there is a purpose. We just can't know it. Everything is "gathered up" in Christ, Ephesians says, as are all the things of the universe, the rocks and birds and trees, and we are, too, all of us are gathered together. It's just that this ecology, this web, is more complex than we can possibly imagine.

"Who has measured the waters in the hollow of his hand," Isaiah asks, "and marked off the heavens with a span?"

One summer I managed to live-trap seven small Douglas squirrels—chickarees—a little bigger than a chipmunk.

A mother had gotten into the walls, and I can tell you that when a chickaree gets into the walls, it doesn't sound like a mouse. It's not a tapping or a scrabbling. It's more like an excavating. It's like small, insistent work. Sometimes they gallop like tiny horses, sprinting down the wide, flat expanse of the attic floor.

A mother, then her babies, in the soft pink nesting of the insulation. Later, juveniles.

So what you do is put a dollop of peanut butter on the

flat metal tongue in the middle of the trap—a long, narrow, wire cage—and when the chickaree tries to take the peanut butter, the spring beneath the tongue snaps and the door of the cage slams, and suddenly there's a small, frantic animal banging and banging against the cage in your attic. You can hear it all over the house.

When you climb up to retrieve the trap, it smells like fear. You can actually smell it, sharp and rank.

Seven times. Dark, bright eyes. Feverish.

Wear gloves. Put a towel over the cage. Drag it across the plywood laid over the insulation and the soft spots in the ceiling between the two-by-fours and walk down the ladder backwards. Drive down the hill to the other side of the highway, on the edge of the hay fields—this is better at night, in the darkness—put the trap on the ground, and slowly open the door.

Usually they streak away. A quick, dark flash. But sometimes they turn and run back through your legs. They're confused. Brace yourself. Hold very still.

It just takes a second, and they're gone.

There is light and there is darkness, and we can't reduce one to the other or see for ourselves how they are held together, what larger movement reconciles their tensions, or if the tension itself is the order, or the plan. For us it must be *and*, this *and* that. To try to rise above the *and*, to turn it into a *thus* or *therefore*, is arrogant. It's impossible.

At the Sea of Galilee I looked out over the waters, to the hills, and the sky, and I saw what our Lord himself must have seen, the same topography, the same rises and falls.

And in Nazareth I saw this: a middle-aged man walking with his son. The son was fifteen or sixteen, with wild eyes and a wild smile, neck straining, head at a crooked angle, stumbling and twitching down the sidewalk. Flapping his arms.

I looked away, as we do. I didn't want to see it—not there, in Nazareth.

But later I remembered. I remembered how patiently the father managed to get the boy into a car. I remembered how heroic the father seemed, and how terribly burdened.

And I believe in the dove, too, descending from the sky. I believe in the wind blowing against the door. I believe the man who wept over Jerusalem entered into it, and let it enter into him, and we must, too, and when we do, when we feel what we must feel, we will rise with him and we will live with him and somehow, in the midst of this sadness and loss, there is joy, too, joy we can't explain and don't have to because it's real, it exists, it's true.

All of it. All at once.

———

Nights and days, bless the Lord! cries the book of Daniel. *Light and darkness, bless the Lord!* *All you beasts, wild and tame, bless the Lord!*

A mother duck squawking and stumbling on the water, the dogs excited in the brush, and there, sure enough, as I push back one frond and then another, the clutch of perfect, deliberate eggs—thirteen of them, pale and smooth, the nest a wreath of knitted fern as soft and dark as the inside of a jewelry box.

As I walk along the shore, talking to myself, a pair of seals starts following my progress.

They poke up in the surf, dive, and poke up again further down, sleek and shiny and smooth, whiskery faces curious, intent. Eyes: bright black.

And once, as I shout and fling open my arms, caught up in my own argument, they pause, turn, and look right at each other. A whole beat. Bobbing.

I swear they're thinking: Is he talking to *us*?

God is not to be "investigated," St. Ephrem says, but "savored." To understand Scripture, we have to stop "prying" into its mysteries and efface ourselves before the glory of it, reading with what he calls the "luminous eye" of imagination and faith.

What do we dream when we dream of opening a door or walking up a flight of stairs? What do we see with our luminous eye? "Rebuke your thought," Ephrem writes. "Beware lest you depict in your mind something conjured up by your own intellect. Let the true Child be depicted."

"In this quest to seek and find God in all things," Pope Francis said in his first interview as pope, "there is still an area of uncertainty:

*there must be. If a person says that he met God with total
certainty and is not touched by a margin of uncertainty,
then this is not good. . . . If one has the answers to all the*

questions—that is proof that God is not with him. It means that he is a false prophet using religion for himself. . . . You must leave room for the Lord, not for certainties. We must be humble. Uncertainty is in every true discernment that is open to finding confirmation in spiritual consolation.

The room where we slept jutted out above the waves, the kelp beds lifting and falling beneath our open window.

And as we woke and stretched, the gray whales fed not a hundred yards away, one, two, now three dark backs arcing and sinking along the shore, like three enormous roommates, calmly observing their morning routine.

The air tastes of coffee and brine.

Just above the rim of the cup, a great fluke slips down the endless hall.

CHAPTER 9

Remembering These Things Are Mysteries

I have been wanting to say how beautiful I think the blueberries are, and precious, and soft. They are like the beads of a rosary, except they give when you touch them, they keep falling away, and they are food for the birds and food for us, and they are countless—there are hundreds and thousands of them hidden in the leaves.

And this one is for me. And this one. Through all the stages of its pushing and its striving, this one berry in its fullness has fallen to me. It bursts in my mouth.

No one is more important than anyone else. No one less. The old man and the child, the lover and the object of love, the young girls on the beach, shrugging off their sweatshirts and shaking out their hair.

The young girls on the beach, laughing now and joining hands, running out towards the waves. About to be beautiful.

Once there was a boy who lived in a desert where the only trees that grew were thorn trees, hard, twisted, brittle things that never bore fruit. And there weren't many of these. Mostly what the boy could see were rocks and sand and the lizards that skittered over them.

When the boy became a man, he went on a journey, and he journeyed through cities and towns and along rivers. And one day he came to a forest, a forest of fir trees and spruce trees, with trunks and tops you had to crane your neck to see, and beneath them the maple and the oak, and beneath them the hazel and the ferns—green and growing things everywhere, in profusion. But all the man could see were thorns.

That's what he knew. There were more of them than he'd seen before, and they were bunched close together. But the man was too tired and hungry to notice how different they were, one from the other. Thorns. That's all they were to him.

Now once, in a village along the way, the people had taken the man in and fed him and told him their stories. That night, by the fire, the Wise Woman of the village had looked him in the eye and said, "One day you will come to a thing we call *the forest*, and here is what you will find. Listen, for what I am about to say will help you." But the man had only smiled politely. Inside he was thinking, That's just what these people think. I don't need them. I think for myself. I see what I see. And so it was.

It was cold that night, but the man hadn't made a fire from branches before—the thorns wouldn't burn. And he was hungry. He could almost have eaten the clods of dirt he walked upon, as now and then he had in the desert. He didn't notice the apple tree growing behind him, a great, branching tree full of round, golden apples. He could smell their lovely apple scent, but he thought it was just perfume. He could see the shining globes of fruit, but he thought that these were just odd, distorted thorns. All he'd ever seen were thorns. All he knew were thorns.

And the night wore on and the man lay down on the cold, uncaring ground. And in the morning, he was dead.

And all around him the birds flew back and forth from branch to branch, and the bees hummed, and the apples and the cherries kept dropping to the ground, the pears and the currants and the plums, softly and sweetly, *plop, plop, plop* onto all the verdant carpets of fern.

We can only discern what is given to us in the moment, right now, and tomorrow we can only act in the moment, and the next.

A man sits across from me at a Mexican restaurant in downtown Spokane and tells me the story of the dying of his wife. We're the same age. We've established that. He's a software engineer. I'm a teacher and a deacon. In a steady, insistent monotone, as if he's standing at the head of a conference table, he tells me the number of breaths his wife took those last few hours and how the number progressively declined: 36 breaths a minute, 24 breaths a minute, 12 breaths a minute.

The next day Bob will get on a plane and fly back to Philadelphia, and I'll get in my car and drive back to Corvallis, and we'll never see each other again, never think about our conversation.

But that doesn't mean the moment doesn't matter.

Bob is lean and trim—I can tell he works out—and he has an expensive haircut, and he wears a crisp, white, tailored shirt, and he doesn't start to cry until the end, when he's talking about going through his wife's clothes and giving them to the poor. There's no point in wasting them, he says.

But then he went home, and he climbed the stairs, and he walked into their bedroom.

That's when he started to cry, across the table from me. At the words *empty closet*.

"Never try to get things too clear," says Friedrich von Hügel. "In this mixed-up life there is always an element of unclearness. . . . If I could understand religion as I understand that two and two make four, it would not be worth understanding."

Augustine's equation in *The Confessions* is different, but the idea is the same: "I wanted to be just as certain about things which I could not see as I was certain that seven and three make ten." But he couldn't be certain—not of Christ, who is too tender, and loving, and fleeting.

"In your book were written all the days that were formed for me," says Psalm 139. But how this is possible, how in the vastness of the universe we can matter at all, no one understands: "How weighty to me are your thoughts," Lord. "How vast is the sum of them!"

"I try to count them—they are more than the sand; / I come to the end—I am still with you."

———

Standing in line at the coffee shop, all we talk about is the weather.

Cold enough for you? We sure could use some rain.

But what else should we talk about? What could be more important than the clouds, or simpler, or more beautiful? Or the wind or the rain? In fact, nothing is more important than walking to the window and looking at the sky and remembering we have bodies. That we live and we die.

This is why we talk about the weather: because there's nothing we can do about it. Because the light, it comes and it goes. Because the clouds are now streaming in, and they're moving above us, tearing over the rooftops and the trees.

To talk about the weather is to be in solidarity with everyone else who talks about the weather. We are all bleary, after all, and empty and dull, waiting for our morning lattes, and who knows what waits for us, down the long corridors and in the lonely rooms? What indifferent voices? What flickering screens?

Moses wanted to see God face to face, but God said, No, no one can see me and live. But here's what I will do. I will put you in this cleft in the rock, and I will put my hand over the cleft, and I will run past you shouting my name—I AM! I AM!—and at the last moment, when I take my hand away, you will see what you will see.

This is why we talk about the weather: out of humility. Because the wind and the rain are all that we can bear.

I am protecting you, and you are protecting me, from our terrible loneliness. Our terrible grief.

———

The call isn't to a grand career or a great adventure. We don't have to go looking.

In the *Spiritual Exercises*, Ignatius gives us tools for making the big decisions in our lives. But first we must make ourselves ready, and to make ourselves ready we must empty ourselves out. Our first call is to be like the birds and the flowers. Our first call is not to worry.

"Jesus is so defined by his faithful obedience to God," Luke Timothy Johnson says, "that he is free to be available to whatever presents itself. Nowhere in ancient literature do we find an equally accessible character." He simply walks through the world and says what he says. He talks to everyone. "Jesus is never distracted." He "mostly seems to respond to what presents itself to him."

What good does it do to rise early and go to bed late at night, "eating the bread of anxious toil"? What good does any of our frantic work do us, Psalm 127 asks, when the Lord "pours down his blessings on us as we slumber"?

This is how it is with the Kingdom of God, the Gospel of Mark says: a man scatters seed on the land, and he goes to sleep and rises night and day, and the seed "sprouts and grows he knows not how."

"The earth produces of itself, first the stalk, then the head, then the full grain in the head."

To say that joy is a seed, to say that faith is a seed, is to say that it grows. It evolves. It just happens.

We're trying to get into Sue's computer, but we can't because she's dead. We don't know the password.

Just last week I was sitting across from her at the Thai restaurant, and I could have asked her and she would have told me. How little would have been required to cross that threshold. A breath. A movement of the tongue. A sound.

Walking in the forest today, down the road, I found a long, smooth tail feather from a hawk, gray and black and dirty white. I brought it home with me.

I like how hard and stiff the quill is, like bone, and yet how light, too, how hollow. Holding it, you think of flight—though you also think of Dante and Shakespeare and Keats, dipping it in ink and starting to write.

———

To say "I'm spiritual but not religious," that I have beliefs and feelings but I don't belong to anything or act in any particular way: it's not possible. We're never outside a religion—a culture—a life. We're never without rules. It's just that some are invisible. It's just that some we choose and some we're sucked up in.

To say we're spiritual but not religious is to say we want to escape from how mundane and ordinary our lives really are, and boring and messy. It's to say we don't want to suffer. It's to refuse to sit at the table with Jesus. To eat with the tax collectors.

And who can blame us? Abstractions are grand, and abstractions are easy. Particulars are humble, and particulars are hard—we have to make choices, and they often don't work out. "Between the idea / And the reality / . . . Falls the Shadow," T. S. Eliot says. Better to stay with ideas.

But we can only find Jesus at table, in Emmaus, with the two dusty, discouraged disciples, and at the breaking of the bread he vanishes. At the moment we finally recognize him, he disappears, and we're left in a Mexican restaurant in downtown Spokane, among the voices and the clattering of the dishes. Someone dropping a spoon.

There are four possible sites for Emmaus in the Holy Land, and at the one we went to, in a dusty field among stones, a stray dog wandered in as we were having mass, a small cattle dog, mottled gray, wagging its stubby tail. The wedding at Cana was an ordinary wedding, in a ragged town, clogged now with cars and cell-phone kiosks and fast-food falafel. We married couples in the group had twenty minutes to renew our vows before the next group came crowding in, there in that cramped little church, and it was hot and noisy, and I looked at Barb and realized how tired she was, and how tired I was.

It was ordinary water Jesus turned into wine, and it was ordinary wine, and nobody saw it or knew it. This is the first miracle?

As Ruth Burrows puts it, "Divine love meets us in this real world and nowhere else: in this moment; in this circumstance, painful and humiliating though it may be: in this person; in the daily unexciting round of seeming trivialities which afford no measure of self-glorification. Divine love meets us here in our flawed, suffering, human condition, and nowhere else."

The very raggedness of the church is revelatory.

I walk down the street, and sunlight is splashing on the stones. Pilgrims flow like a river. I stop and have a cappuccino, and I think, This is how it is. The mind is Rome, as Freud said. Is a city, with layers. Churches everywhere, built with marble they stripped from the Forum, and underneath them the crumbling cities of the dead.

It's dark down there, and close, and warm. The woman who is leading us has a strange accent. There are chambers and clues and symbols they've exposed with toothbrushes. The woman leads us on, singsonging, until finally we reach the tomb where the bones of St. Peter lie, a few narrow, flat bones, like leftover short ribs, sheathed now in a plastic tube on the dusty ledge where they were found, walled up in the foundations, directly beneath the great, high altar.

This is where we've been going. This is all that's left of him.

I think of the birds I have known.

There was the Swainson's in the thicket, the one I saw sing, head thrown back, throat bubbling, high above the water. There was the Wilson's in the thicket, the same thicket: a little canary on a branch, head cocked, looking right at me. There was the common yellowthroat along the road, two days in a row—the same one, I think—flitting in the alder screens, its slick black mask like a bandit's. I swear he knew me.

Or by the ocean, on the point, high above the only water I've seen you could actually call aquamarine, and endlessly, all the way to the horizon, and there, on the branch of an old-growth spruce crowding the edge of the trail, big as a dog, a bald eagle, so unmoving you think at first it must be a statue of an eagle, animatronic. But no, the clear yellow eyes blink, they click, and the snowy head turns on the flange of the neck, very slowly, and the people are walking by and talking, and then see it, and then stop, and point, and exclaim—and then, on this sunny day above the sea, start passing back word of it, person to person, down the trail, each one in turn handing on what has been handed on to them—*an eagle!*—all the way back to the curve where I am just now coming out into the open.

———

Pema Chodron talks about being tired out and fed up, "the experience of complete hopelessness," and she explains that in Buddhism this is a good thing, "the beginning of the beginning":

Without giving up hope—that there's somewhere better to be, that there's someone better to be—we will never relax with where we are or who we are. To think that we can finally get it all together is unrealistic. To seek for some lasting security is futile.

And this is a Christian idea, too.

Christianity rests on two premises.

The first is that God is present in every moment and in every molecule, that his grace and his love are nowhere less than complete and full, anywhere in the universe, anywhere in time. What's happening here and now is as holy and as beautiful as anything that has ever happened or ever will. To deny this is to say that God is not God.

The second premise is that the love of God and the grace of God are freely given, are nothing but gift, that there's nothing we can ever do to earn them and nothing we have to do. No matter how much I read or pray or do good works, I will never be more loved by God than I am in this very second. Yes, we should strive to be better, we should strive to be more moral and faithful people, but not in order to merit the love of God but rather as a loving and grateful response to it.

"Abandon all hope ye who enter here," says the famous inscription on the gate to Dante's Inferno. But in a way this is also the inscription on the gate to heaven.

Birds never think about the future or worry about it, and they don't have to, because the present is enough and more than enough. "Therefore I tell you," Jesus says in the Sermon on the Mount, "do not worry about your life, what you will eat or what you will drink." The birds neither sow nor reap, they do not gather into barns, and yet our heavenly Father feeds them.

We can give up hope because we already have everything we need: we have Christ.

In Christ from the beginning of time God has transcended all time. God isn't linear as we are, isn't stuck on a timeline, as we are. Jesus's call is to a radical surrender in the present moment, is to give up worry and to trust in him, and when we do, when we enter into this freedom and this playfulness and this joy, we are already experiencing eternal life.

When we get to heaven, we will recognize it.

St. Ignatius calls this the idea of "indifference," not in the sense that we don't care about anything but that we care about everything, equally. It's at the heart of Ignatian spirituality, "The Principle and Foundation": that all things on earth are created for the purpose of helping us attain our end, which is to serve God; that we must therefore use these things "to the extent" that they help us towards this end, and for the same reason "rid" ourselves of them "in so far as" they prevent us from this; and that, in short, "we must make ourselves indifferent . . . we should not prefer health or sickness, riches to poverty, honor to dishonor, a long life to a short one," because in all things God is reaching out to us, and in all things nothing else matters but praising him and reverencing him and serving him. Whatever happens, we already have everything we need.

————

One Sunday after mass I'm asked to talk to the little kids at religious education, three years old to first grade. When I'm done, I get a lot of questions—"Is Jesus a ghost?" "If Jesus is in heaven with my grandma, how can he be down here, too?"—questions not unlike the questions of biblical scholars.

But I didn't need to answer. One little girl jumped in, perfectly happy, and said that Jesus is everywhere, all around us, and everybody nodded. Then a little blonde boy raised his hand and said, "You know what? My mom made blueberry pancakes this morning!"

And somehow that seemed to follow. It made perfect sense.

When an idea or a feeling comes from God, William Barry says, it has a certain resonance. It's striking. It's like the feeling we have when we're reading a book and a passage hits us as true and right. It's in boldface.

When an idea or feeling comes from God, it has a certain clarity and persistence. We don't forget it. It sticks with us, and it keeps coming up, again and again. It doesn't go away.

And third and most important, Barry says, when an idea or feeling comes from God, it's accompanied by joy and peace to varying degrees. It lifts our hearts—we feel good, like ourselves—even if later we begin to question and doubt again, as we always do.

The sheep hear the voice of the shepherd directly, in the image from John's Gospel, and they follow it. But these feelings we have are the voice of the shepherd, too, these feelings of resonance and clarity and joy.

"It seems as though these thoughts come to me," Barry says, "and I know that what I am experiencing is different from when I am talking to myself."

Behind the Monastery of St. Gertrude's, the Stations of the Cross climb a forested hill, fourteen of them, plaster scenes with wooden frames and shingled roofs like small, flat houses spread out along a path on the way to the top.

But they begin in an orchard, a cherry orchard, and when I was there, it was harvest time.

Jesus Condemned for Us, the first station read, in Gothic, the Lord before Pilate, white as frosting, the crowd on either side, standing in line.

Above them all a cherry tree, the hanging branches thick with fruit.

Bright red fistfuls of Bings.

"The Spirit himself bears witness with our spirit that we are children of God," Paul says in Romans. But this dis-

cernment only happens in the moment. It's a discernment
of moments. It happens day to day.

I break bread with the dying man and sleep in the dying
man's house, and in the morning before the sun rises, I sit
with him at table and drink the coffee he has made, chatting
about ordinary things.

At first we are surrounded by darkness. The breakfast
lights shine, and the window looking out to the sea and all
the storms becomes a mirror in which all we can see are ourselves, our cups, our faces.

But the surf booms in the distance. We can hear it. And
gradually the light seeps back, and we can see the edges of
trees and the waves cresting beyond the mouth of the river,
just as we knew we would. The wide sea. The sky.

It was always there, the dying man says. It's the world.
The enormous world.

*Therefore I tell you, do not worry about your life, what you
will eat or what you will drink.*

I am the bread. I am the Bread of Life.
Whoever comes to me will never hunger. Never die.

Juan has come late to mass again, wandering over from
the retirement center next door. He can't seem to remember
what time it is.

I'm unsnapping my alb—everyone else is gone—but,
grudgingly, I bring him over to the tabernacle, open the two
small metal doors, and remove the Body of Christ.

And when I reach out to put the host on his tongue, before he receives, he turns his smooth, brown, ancient head and kisses me on the inside of the arm.

In the crook.

CHAPTER 10

Completing Creation

"The universe took 13.7 billion years to produce this amazing book," John Mather says, on the cover of Michael Dowd's *Thank God for Evolution.*

Of course.

It took the universe 13.7 billion years to produce this amazing chair.

It took the universe 13.7 billion years to produce this amazing pen.

It took the universe 13.7 billion years to produce that amazing rhododendron outside my window, and the winter wren overflowing in that rhododendron, that amazing, bubbling winter wren, overflowing, not to mention my ears, which hear it, and my eyes, which see it.

It seems that life is "almost indecently eager to evolve eyes," Richard Dawkins says. The compound eye of an insect or a prawn, he says, "or camera eyes like ours or a squid's, . . . [or] parabolic reflector eyes like those of a limpet." This is all going somewhere, in other words. It's cumulative. It's purposeful. It's always coming to a point.

"It takes an entire Universe to make an apple pie," Carl Sagan says. It takes an entire universe to make a banana split, with whipped cream and a cherry on top. It takes an entire universe to make a crazy cake, the way Mom used to, before she died. No eggs. Just thumb three wells into the cocoa and the flour, then pour oil into the first well, vinegar into the second, and vanilla into the third. Stir, bake, let cool, and frost with vanilla frosting. Oh, how I loved it! I couldn't stop eating.

Stars had to explode to produce the ingredients. Eons for the wheat. Think of the skies above the fields and the color of the skies.

Think of the winter wren: two-thirds of its body is devoted to the production of song. It's such a tiny thing, it weighs barely an ounce, but inside that feathery body the bones hollow and the lungs expand and the melody and purity of that song keep bubbling and pouring out. Amazing.

The wren is merely a space, an emptiness, through which song is produced. It is otherwise hardly even there.

What good does it do the world if we pray the *examen*—if we sit in a room at the end of a day and remember the darkness and remember the light? What lasting difference does it make if we smile at the barista or hold open the door? If we write the long email but decide not to send it? What value is it to the people in our lives if we spend the morning writing a poem, or walking in the woods, or weeding the front flowerbed?

What worth is our joy?

A worth beyond price. "A thought," Teilhard de Chardin says, "a material improvement, a unique nuance of human love, the enchanting complexity of a smile or glance—the spiritual success of the universe is bound up with the release of every possible energy in it." We say a kind word, we sit and remember and reflect, and nobody sees this, nobody knows, but a love is released, a momentary goodness, and it joins with the love and creativity and energy released by all the other thoughts and acts and feelings going on every minute, every second, and these come together and gather force. Evolution is still going on, the universe is still growing and expanding, and everything is becoming more intricate, more complex.

"We serve to complete the work of creation," Teilhard says, "even by the humblest work of our hands."

One Monday morning as I walked back from campus to the parish, I happened to see the church janitor sweeping the sidewalk on the other side of the parking lot. I was coming around a corner, so I could see him but he couldn't see me. There was no one else around, except for a big, shaggy man sitting on the curb next to a shopping cart crammed with bottles and cans. It was just the two of them, the maintenance man and the homeless man, and what the maintenance man did was say good morning. He said good morning and chatted for a few minutes, a friendly hi-how-are-you as he kept sweeping up the leaves. He didn't have to. He could have ignored the man or asked him to get out of the way. But he didn't. He worked around him. He swept the walk and chatted about the weather, and the homeless man looked up from beneath his long, stringy hair, and nodded and said *Yes*, like anyone else. *Lovely sun.*

Just a moment. When no one was looking.

Before we pray, Anthony de Mello says, we should "seek

this disposition: that we embark upon this exercise not for ourselves alone but for the welfare of creation, of which we are a part, and that any transformation we experience will redound to the benefit of the world."

This is the hardest thing to believe, and the most freeing. That what we think and feel matters. That the inner life is as real as the outer, and finally even more so. That somehow we are all connected.

———

God comes to Julian of Norwich holding out "a little thing" like a nut, a hazelnut, something small and round and hard, and looking at it, Julian is confused. What is this?

God answers, "It is all that is made."

All that is made? How can that be, Julian asks, "for it seems it might suddenly have sunk into nothing because of its littleness."

And then she is answered again: "It lasts and ever shall, because God loves it."

In *The Exercises*, Ignatius says, "In those who are making spiritual progress, the action of the good angel is gentle, light, and sweet, as a drop of water entering a sponge." But the action of "the evil spirit," on the other hand, "is sharp, noisy, and disturbing, like a drop of water falling upon a rock."

How do we know a feeling comes from God? Because it is small.

But not just compression—expansion: God becomes a

child in the womb of a young girl, and the child is born and the child becomes a man, and when that man dies and when he rises again, the fire that breaks from him then, as Gerard Manley Hopkins puts it, is "a billion times told lovelier."

From the tiniest seed grows the mustard tree, the largest of all the trees. From the wheat that swells as we sleep comes the harvest, "some a hundredfold, some sixty, some thirty."

At the end of each day there's the story we can tell of our accomplishments and conquests and awards. But then there's the real story, and it's the small story, the story of the fleeting, the intangible. The ordinary. The real.

Because my mother died suddenly and unexpectedly, we weren't prepared, and what made it harder is how bitter and unhappy she was, at the end of her life and all of her life.

This was in Spokane, where I grew up. Mom died on a Friday, we drove up that Saturday, and on Monday we were coming back through the Gorge on I-84. We had passed the Dalles and were heading towards Hood River, as the hills start to get forested again. It was sunny and beautiful. The light was on the water.

We came around a bend, and there was Mount Hood, the first time you can see it clearly, white against the blue of the sky, half-hidden by clouds, and all at once I was flooded with a feeling of joy, of deep joy, and also of something like excitement and anticipation, as if something wonderful was about to happen and already had. It was completely unexpected and, in a way, completely inappropriate.

Luke tells us the disciples are filled with "great joy" when Jesus ascends into the clouds. They are intensely happy after he leaves. But then, before this, Jesus had risen from the dead and had done all these miraculous things, and the Holy Spirit was about to come.

My mother was dead. She was gone. I thought, Wait— I'm not supposed to feel this.

Except the joy didn't seem to be coming *from* me. It seemed to be flowing *into* me. It seemed to be in the air and in the water and in the trees, it seemed to be all around me, in the world, in the light, and somehow it was coming into me, too. It was flooding me. Filling me.

Brothers and sisters, the writer of Ephesians says, may "the eyes of your hearts [be] enlightened" so "you may know what is the hope to which he has called you, what are the riches of his glorious inheritance among the saints, and what is the immeasurable greatness of his power for us who believe." That's how it was, for a moment, hope and glory and surpassing greatness. It didn't last long—but it was there, something happened, and I think it was like the Ascension, an experience of the fullness of the one who "fills all things," as Ephesians later says.

What happens in the Ascension is that Jesus is no longer localized. He is no longer stuck in a particular time and place. Jesus ascends "so that he can fill all things," Ephesians also says. He ascends into the heavens and fills all the heavens and all the earth. His spirit is everywhere, infusing every speck of matter and particle of light and so infusing us, too. It's a cosmic vision and an ecological one, both incredibly vast and wonderfully intimate, and it has to do with both this life and the one to come.

And I thought, Maybe this is why the disciples were able

to do the things they did after Jesus ascended, why they showed such courage and hope in the face of hardship. Because they felt this.

The story isn't over. It's never over. There's something greater still, and we are all a part of it, every one of us.

This experience, as I say, could have been a delusion or some kind of wish fulfillment. But I tell you, the surprise of it and the joy of it were in part the feeling that my mother—my mother, of all people—was at peace and was at home, and somehow it was her, or it was God telling me through her, that we can all be at peace, we can all be at home.

"Don't think that union lies in being very close to God," St. Teresa of Avila says. "For those, too, who offend him are close, although they may not want to be."

This is what I think my mother's death was teaching me—that "the best help for holding on to the light," as St. Teresa puts it, "is to understand that we can do nothing and that it comes from God."

But more than that.

Because the glory does come. The heavens do open. Suddenly and unexpectedly, whether we deserve it or not, whether I do or my mother does or anyone does, we are all caught up in the story, we are all caught up in the Ascension, we are all caught up in this marvelous light.

———

Year after year they keep track of the birds as they first appear in the spring, writing down what they see in their ledgers. They publish this. You can read these: cinnamon teals and blue-ringed teals and plovers and yellowlegs and terns. Hidden, they see what is hidden; unnoticed, they notice, and they write it all down, as if it matters, as if it makes any difference.

Because it does. Maybe nothing matters more.

Vaux's Swift: *Earliest Arrival Date: 5 April*
            Average Arrival Date: 19 April
            Records Kept: 34 years

Vesper Sparrow: *Earliest Arrival Date: 19 March*
            Average Arrival Date: 12 April
            Records Kept: 15 years

Eastern kingbirds, western kingbirds, vireos—warbling, Cassin's, red-eyed—and Nashville warblers and yellow warblers and black-throated grays and birds I didn't know we had, didn't know came through here, from wherever they come, here in the valley where I walk and look out at the rooftops and the hills one morning when the cherry trees are blossoming and there is a haze in the air like fall.

And not just their coming but their going. Their going is recorded, too, day by day and hour by hour.

Like the Swainson's thrushes, my favorite birds, for their lovely, throaty song, their deep summer song. They leave, too. They stop singing and they nest and they raise their young, and in the fall they fly away, back to the Amazon, to the jungles, flying away at night, in the darkness, beneath the bright, full moon, and you can hear this, if you're listening, you can hear the thrushes whitting above you, in the sky. *Weep, weep, weep.*

From: Floyd
Date: Friday, August 31, 10:58 pm
At this moment (10:58 pm Aug. 31) apparently a wave of Swainson's Thrushes is flowing over my part of McMinnville under the bright full moon. I'm hearing their calls almost simultaneously from many different directions.

From: Bill
Date: Sat, Sep 1, 1:38 am
There they were—Swainson's Thrushes, calling softly while winging south against tonight's beautiful, bright blue moon. What a sweet sound, so full of longing, promise, and the sadness of another summer almost gone. Merry Fall Migration!

Merry fall. To love not just the coming but the going. To watch for the leaving, and to know it, and to greet it—to walk out into the night and hear it—apparently a wave of thrushes, flowing over us, calling softly while winging south, *weep, weep, weep,* against the bright blue moon.

———

"I have said these things to you," Jesus tells his disciples, "so that my joy may be in you and that your joy may be complete."

But this is the night before the Crucifixion, this is the

Farewell Discourse in the Gospel of John, and sadness fills the room. Fear.

How can joy be possible?

O Lord, when I think of the galaxies and the stars, I am afraid.

When I try to imagine the distances, I am defeated, I am lost.

And yet the Scriptures say you know me and love me by name. The Gospels say you follow the flight and the fall of every sparrow.

And the warblers? I could crush one with my hand.

And yet when they return in the spring, and I hear them in the trees, I rejoice and am glad.

Is this how it is for you, my God? Do you delight in me as I delight in them, when I hear them sing again?

In the beginning of John, Jesus says we must be "born again," but now he changes the image. He says, "When a woman is in labor she has pain, because her hour has come. But when her child is born, she no longer remembers the anguish because of the joy of having brought a human being into the world."

And so, "you have pain now, but I will see you again, and your hearts will rejoice, and no one will take your joy from you."

Not birth: labor. Not a child anymore. The mother.

O Lord, may I sing, and may we all sing, and when we fall, may we fall into the vastness of your love.

May we die into your distances.

Scanning the wood violets along the trail for the leash I lost, all I see are the wood violets, and the columbine, and the wild iris, fragile and unfurling.

And the hazel, and the thimbleberry, and all the fresh new green—and high against the tops of the firs, the white crowns of the blossoming cherry trees, as sweet as clouds.

As brief.

This is the root of the word *relic*: *to abandon, to leave behind.*

O Lord, when the morning star hangs in the oak tree, I rejoice and am glad.

Though just a little, I admit, as it's early, and I'm groggy, and the star wavers and blurs as if through water, and my seeing of it depends on the orbit and tilt of two planets I am absolutely sure know me not, spinning in space inconceivably far apart, without intelligence or regard.

Still, some branches of the oak *do* bend, horizontally, like the edges around the spaces where puzzle pieces go, and for a moment the star *does* glow, in the middle of the wavy frame the branches make, soft and beautiful, it seems to me, from my angle, and the air is soft, too, and cool, for the first time all this summer long. Every morning the sky darkens more and more.

O God, the first leaves of the maple are even starting to turn!

And though I will have forgotten this by midday, or sooner—by my second cup of coffee—what thrills in me for just a moment is the sure and certain knowledge that, whatever else, the blessed days are growing shorter.

———

We bought the tree with the money I made when I baptized Stan, who had nineteen confirmed kills in Vietnam. He's an old man now, in a wheelchair, shriveled and pale, and he wanted to be cleansed of his sins. "I've been in hell," he told me, "and I want to be free." And though he couldn't talk much, and could hardly move, when I started to pour the water on his head, and I began to say the words "I baptize you in the name of the Father"—"and of the Son," he said, "and of the Holy Spirit," and the water dribbled down his face and dripped off his chin, wetting the front of his pale, checked shirt.

We planted the tree on a fine spring day. The earth was soft and warm. We dug the hole, scored the matted roots, and gently set it in, then filled the hole with amended soil and watered, thoroughly, soaking the ground until the bed had turned to mud.

It's a pretty tree. A paperbark maple, they call it, because the bark peels off in curly strips almost smooth enough to write on.

Prayer as Autobiography

The Spiritual Exercises began with a wound.

Ignatius Loyola was a soldier first, in sixteenth-century Spain, and he started to think about prayer and discernment as he was recovering from a leg wound he received in the Battle of Pamplona in 1521. He limped the rest of his life.

Over years of prayer and study and travel, he developed *The Spiritual Exercises* into a training manual for the Society of Jesus, the religious order he founded, and it's become an important guide for many others.

"The *examen* of conscience" begins the text and guides it.

Examen is Spanish for *examination*. If we can pray in no other way, Ignatius says, we should pray like this. By examining our lives. By remembering:

1. *The first point is to render thanks to God for the favors we have received.*
2. *The second point is to ask for the grace to know my sins and to free myself from them.*
3. *The third point is to demand an account of my soul from the moment of rising until the present examination; either hour*

    by hour or from one period to another. I shall first make an
    examination of my thoughts, then my words. . . .

4. *The fourth point is to ask pardon of God our Lord for my*
    failings.

5. *The fifth point is to resolve to amend my life with the help of*
    God's grace. Close with the "Our Father."

Implied in these five "points" are the three movements that organize this book.

Trusting Joy is implied in the first and third points, when we give thanks for the "favors" we receive in a day and give an "account" even "hour by hour" of what's happened to us.

Facing Darkness is obvious in the three middle steps, when we think about how we have failed and ask God for forgiveness.

Seeing God in Everything is suggested by Ignatius's fifth point, "to resolve to amend my life with the help of God's grace," and by his instruction to conclude with the Our Father: "give us this day," "lead us not into temptation." Once we recall the presence of God, we resolve to act in the world ourselves, to serve the people around us, discerning as best we can the promptings of the Spirit.

The rest of *The Exercises* is taken up by a number of directed meditations, five or six a day, grounded in Scripture and carefully sequenced over four weeks. This is the Long Retreat, or the Thirty-Day Retreat, or the Silent Retreat, and the *examen* is central to the experience. Retreatants are directed to pray the *examen* at least twice a day, and all the other exercises are based on its assumptions.

Two later sections of *The Exercises* are also important for understanding the *examen.*

In "Making a Choice of a Way of Life," Ignatius lays out guidelines for deciding whether to join the priesthood or get married or change professions, though for him our first vocation isn't to career but to living with hope in the present moment.

In "The Discernment of Spirits" he provides "rules" for distinguishing "the different movements produced in the soul," whether from evil impulses or from the Spirit. This, too, is a day-to-day process, requiring both humility and a degree of doubt—not about God, but about our knowledge of God.

As Ignatius says in the "Suscipe," or what's also called the Prayer of St. Ignatius, "Take, O Lord, and receive all my liberty, my memory, my understanding, and my entire will, and all that I have and possess." In the end, all we can do is surrender.

Everything in the *examen* flows from a syllogism in the beginning of *The Exercises* and can be seen as a way of putting it into practice. Ignatius calls this "The Principle and Foundation":

that we are created to "praise, reverence, and serve God";
that all things in the world are created to help us fulfill
*   this end;*
that we must "therefore" use the things of the world "to the
*   extent" that they will help us attain this end, and rid*

ourselves of these things "in so far as" they prevent us from attaining it.

Ignatius's language is awkward and mechanical, his metaphors often military, drawn from his experience as a soldier, and he seems preoccupied with sin. But underneath all that, throughout *The Exercises*, there is a deep conviction that God is present in our lives, in all our thoughts and actions.

When we reflect on our experience, we become aware of God.

Prayer is autobiography.

Chapter Notes

....

Unless otherwise indicated, biblical quotations are from the New Revised Standard Version.

Quotations from The Spiritual Exercises *are from the translation by Anthony Mottola (New York: Doubleday, 1964, 1989).*

Preface

xii   *"Maybe whatever seems / to be so"* . . . William Stafford, "Simple Talk," in *Oregon Message* (New York: Harper & Row, 1987), p. 70.

xiii   *"The believer is essentially"* . . . Pope Francis, *The Joy of the Gospel* (New York: Image, 2013), p. 14.

xiii   *"I have said these things to you"* . . . John 15:11.

xiv   *The details are simple* . . . C. H. Dodd, *Parables of the Kingdom* (New York: Scribner's, 1961), p. 5. See also James Martin, *Jesus: A Pilgrimage* (New York: HarperCollins, 2014), p. 200.

Part I

1 *"The first movement is singing"* . . . Czeslaw Milosz, "The Poor Poet," in *The Collected Poems* (New York: Ecco Press, 1988), p. 60.

Chapter 1

4 *Joy isn't just pleasure* . . . C. S. Lewis, *Surprised by Joy: The Shape of My Early Life* (New York: Harcourt, Brace, 1955), p. 18.

5 *comes to us in a still, small voice* . . . 1 Kings 19:9–13.

5 *we always sink, as Peter does* . . . Matthew 14:22–33.

6 *"God did not dictate the Scriptures"* . . . Robert Barron, "Bill Maher and Biblical Interpretation," www.word onfire.org, June 13, 2014.

6 *The Bible is . . . filtered through human language* . . . *Dei Verbum,* in *Vatican Council II: Constitutions, Decrees, and Declarations,* edited by Austin Flannery, O.P. (Northport, NY: Costello Publishing, 1966), pp. 104–6.

7 *lovely in ten thousand places* . . . I'm echoing Gerard Manley Hopkins, "As Kingfishers Catch Fire," in *The Poems of Gerard Manley Hopkins,* fourth edition, edited by W. H. Gardner and N. H. MacKenzie (New York: Oxford University Press, 1984), p. 90.

7 *Water is always becoming wine* . . . C. S. Lewis, *Miracles* (New York: Touchstone, 1947, 1960), p. 179.

8   *"The Watchful Tree"* ... Jeremiah 1:11-12, New Jerusalem Bible.

9   *"I am only a man"* ... Czeslaw Milosz, "Veni Creator," in *The Collected Poems* (New York: Ecco Press, 1988), p. 194.

11   *"I was blind, now I see"* ... John 9:1-25, 35-36.

11   *The Samaritan woman at the well* ... John 4:4-42.

12   *The Word of God is a seed* ... Matthew 13:1-9.

12   *Adam falls asleep* ... Genesis 2:21.

13   *"This is ... bone of my bones"* ... Genesis 2:23.

13   *a man who sowed seed ... a treasure buried in a field* ... Matthew 13:24-30, 44.

Chapter 2

15   *"My mind ... has become a piece of difficult ground"* ... Augustine, *The Confessions,* translated by Rex Warner (New York: New American Library, 1963), p. 226.

17   *"The hills gird themselves"* ... Psalm 65:13-14.

19   *"Do whatever most kindles love in you"* ... *The Interior Castle,* in *The Collected Works of St. Teresa of Avila*, translated by Kieran Kavanaugh and Otilio Rodriguez (Washington, DC: ICS Publications, 1980), volume II, p. 319.

      The wording in this translation is slightly different: "Do that which best stirs you to love."

21   *"He sanctified the fountains of waters"* . . . Sermon by St.
      Proclus of Constantinople, bishop, "Office of Readings
      for Wednesday, after Epiphany to the Baptism of the
      Lord," in *The Liturgy of the Hours According to the Roman
      Rite*, English translation by the International Commis-
      sion on English in the Liturgy (New York: Catholic Book
      Publishing, 1974), volume I, p. 595.

21   *the Spirit, like a dove, comes down upon him* . . . Matthew
      3:13–17.

21   *tempted by Satan in the wilderness* . . . Matthew 4:1–11.

22   *"he saw . . . the Spirit descending like a dove"* . . . Mark 1:10.

23   *the gospel is always the gospel* according to . . . Lawrence
      Cunningham, *Things Seen and Unseen: A Catholic Theo-
      logian's Notebook* (Notre Dame, IN: Sorin Books, 2010),
      p. 236.

24   *He rejects him three times* . . . Matthew 4:1–11.

25   *Jesus "disregards the message"* . . . This is the way the New
      American Bible translates Mark 5:36.

25   *"Why do you make a commotion and weep?"* . . . Mark 5:39.

26   *"God did not make death"* . . . Wisdom 1:13–15.

Chapter 3

30   *the Beloved Disciple leans back* . . . John 13:25, New Amer-
      ican Bible translation.

31   *Imagine the house where Mary . . . The Spiritual Exercises
        of St. Ignatius,* translated by Anthony Mottola (New York:
        Doubleday, 1964, 1989), p. 69.

32   *"In time of desolation one should never make a change" . . .
        The Spiritual Exercises,* Mottola, p. 130.

33   *After dinner C. S. Lewis and J. R. R. Tolkien are walking . . .*
        See Lewis's letter describing this crucial moment to his
        friend Arthur Greeves, October 18, 1931, in *The Letters
        of C. S. Lewis to Arthur Greeves,* edited by Walter Hooper
        (New York: Macmillan, 1979), p. 193.

33–34   *stealing past . . . the "dragons" of reason . . .* "Sometimes
        Fairy Stories Say Best What's to Be Said," in *On Stories
        and Other Essays on Literature,* edited by Walter Hooper
        (New York: Harcourt, Brace, 1982), p. 47.

36   *"the fruit of the Spirit" . . .* Galatians 5:16–26.

36   *trust your feelings of "consolation" . . . The Spiritual Exer-
        cises,* Mottola, pp. 129, 133.

36   *Diadochus of Photice uses the image . . .* See his treatise
        On Spiritual Perfection, in *The Liturgy of the Hours Ac-
        cording to the Roman Rite,* English translation by the
        International Commission on English in the Liturgy
        (New York: Catholic Book Publishing, 1975), volume
        III, p. 154.

Part II

43   *"One does not become enlightened"* . . . Carl Jung, *Collected Works*, edited by Erhard Adler and R. F. C. Hull (Princeton: Princeton University Press, 2014), volume 13, p. 265.

Chapter 4

45   *"Another word for father"* . . . Li-Young Lee, "Words for Worry," in *Book of My Nights* (Rochester, NY: BOA Editions, 2001).

46   *"My God, my God, why have you forsaken me?"* . . . Mark 15:34.

47   *"Who am I that You should forsake me?"* . . . *Come Be My Light: The Private Writings of the "Saint of Calcutta,"* edited and with commentary by Brian Kolodiejchuk, M.C. (New York: Doubleday, 2007), pp. 186-87.

48   *we begin to "shrivel up"* . . . *to feel like "empty husks"* . . . Ruth Burrows, *The Essence of Prayer* (Mahwah, NJ: HiddenSpring, 2006), pp. 38-39.

49   *"he was sorry to die"* . . . *Come Be My Light*, p. 180.

49   *"The Lord is near to the brokenhearted"* . . . Psalm 34:18.

50   *"All deepened life"* . . . Friedrich von Hügel, *Letters to a Niece* (London: HarperCollins, 1995), p. 56.

51   *Love . . . always fails* . . . I am alluding here to the famous litany in 1 Corinthians 13.

52   *Desolation demonstrates that we shouldn't "claim as our own"* . . . *The Spiritual Exercises of St. Ignatius,* translated by Anthony Mottola (New York: Doubleday, 1964, 1989), p. 131.

53   *"The best proof that it is really God"* . . . Thomas Green, S.J., *When the Well Runs Dry: Prayer beyond the Beginnings* (Notre Dame, IN: Ave Maria Press, 2007), p. 101.

55   *"We have to trust it utterly to God"* . . . Burrows, *The Essence of Prayer,* p. 6.

Chapter 5

57   *"Take, O Lord, and receive"* . . . *The Spiritual Exercises of St. Ignatius,* translated by Anthony Mottola (New York: Doubleday, 1964, 1989), p. 104. *Suscipe* is the Latin word for "receive" or "take."

59   *Our desire is mistaken* . . . I am alluding here to the traditional notion of "mistaken desire." For more on this, see Robert Barron, *The Strangest Way: Walking the Christian Path* (New York: Orbis, 2002), p. 50.

59   *"God's love has been poured into our hearts"* . . . Romans 5:5.

59   *the Samaritan woman at the well* . . . John 4:4-42.

59   *"those who drink of the water"* . . . John 4:14.

60   *a study was published* . . . Timothy Wilson et al., "Just Think: The Challenge of the Disengaged Mind," *Science,* July 4, 2014, pp. 75-77.

60   *like the rain and the snow that come down* . . . Isaiah 55:10.

61   *"As they were going they were cleansed"* . . . This is the New American Bible translation of Luke 17:14–15.

62   *"God is always a surprise"* . . . Pope Francis, in an early interview, published in *America*, September 30, 2013.

62   *For C. S. Lewis joy is a "technical term"* . . . C. S. Lewis, *Surprised by Joy: The Shape of My Early Life* (New York: Harcourt, Brace, 1955), p. 18.

65   *"Should the world go to hell"* . . . Fyodor Dostoevsky, *Notes from Underground,* translated by Richard Katz, in *The Norton Anthology of World Literature, Shorter Third Edition* (New York: W. W. Norton, 1989), volume II, p. 86.

65   *"Which is better, cheap happiness or sublime suffering?"* . . . Dostoevsky, *Notes from Underground*, p. 90.

65   *There's a sadness we all feel* . . . See "Louis C. K. Hates Cell Phones," posted on YouTube, September 20, 2013.

66   *"People will do anything rather than face their own souls"* . . . Carl Jung, *Collected Works,* edited by Erhard Adler and R. F. C. Hull (Princeton: Princeton University Press, 2014), volume 12, p. 136.

67   *"Get up and go on your way"* . . . Luke 17:19.

67   *"If we are faithless"* . . . 2 Timothy 2:12–13.

67   *Peter denies Jesus three times* . . . Mark 14:66–72.

Chapter 6

71   *what he calls our "inner incompetence"* ... Michael Casey,
        Toward God (Ligouri, MO: Triumph Books, 1996), p. 16.

73   *"How great a forest is set ablaze"* ... James 3:5.

73   *"O daughter Babylon"* ... Psalm 137:8-9.

74   *C. S. Lewis even turns his interpretation of Psalm 137* ...
        C. S. Lewis, *Reflections on the Psalms* (New York: Har-
        court, Brace, 1958, 1986), p. 136.

75   *this is called "heightened neurosis"* ... Pema Chodron,
        *The Places That Scare You: A Guide to Fearlessness in Dif-
        ficult Times* (Boston: Shambhala Publications, 2002), pp.
        105-6.

75   *"We never graduate"* ... Michael Casey, *Seventy-Four
        Tools for Good Living: Reflections on the Fourth Chapter
        of Benedict's Rule* (Collegeville, MN: Liturgical Press,
        2014), p. 8.

76   *Pema Chodron recommends three things* ... *Taking the
        Leap: Freeing Ourselves from Old Habits and Fears* (Bos-
        ton: Shambhala Publications, 2012), pp. 39-40.

76   *"I need to overcome a sense of my own impotence"* ... *The
        Duty of Delight: The Journals of Dorothy Day*, edited by
        Robert Ellsberg (New York: Image Books, 2008), p. 63.

77   *"O Lord and master of my life"* ... Day, *The Duty of De-
        light*, p. 693.

78   *"Lord, I have let myself be deceived"* . . . Pope Francis, *The Joy of the Gospel* (New York: Image, 2013), p. 6.

79   *"a long, loving look at the real"* . . . Walter Burghardt, quoted in James Martin, *The Jesuit Guide to (Almost) Everything* (New York: HarperCollins, 2010), p. 86.

79   *"The real I look at"* . . . Walter Burghardt, quoted in Jim Manney, *A Simple Life-Changing Prayer: Discovering the Power of St. Ignatius Loyola's Examen* (Chicago: Loyola Press, 2011), p. 41.

79   *Whenever you're mad at somebody else* . . . Anthony de Mello, *Awareness: The Perils and Opportunities of Reality* (New York: Doubleday, 1990), p. 51.

Chapter 7

83   *an ordained deacon . . . is a "sacramental sign"* . . . See *The Catechism of the Catholic Church* (St. Paul, MN: The Wanderer Press, 1994), 1570: by ordination the deacon is "configure[d] to Christ, who made himself the 'deacon' or servant of all." See also the *National Directory for the Formation, Ministry, and Life of Permanent Deacons* (Washington, DC: United States Conference of Catholic Bishops, 2005), p. 16: deacons are "consecrated witnesses to service."

84   *"The deacon is one who waits"* . . . Mark Santer, "Diaconate and Discipleship," *Theology* 81 (May 1978): 13.

85   *"Is there anything at all that is peculiar to a deacon?"* . . . Santer, "Diaconate and Discipleship," p. 14.

86   *"The paradox at the heart of Christianity"* . . . Dermot
      Lane, *Christ at the Centre* (Mahwah, NJ: Paulist Press,
      1991), p. 111.

87   *Jesus did not deem equality with God "something to be ex-*
      ploited" . . . Philippians 2:6–11.

88   *"We all have to discover"* . . . Jean Vanier, *Becoming Human*
      (Mahwah, NJ: Paulist Press, 1998), pp. 58–59.

88   *"one adorable point of the incredible condescension of the*
      Incarnation" . . . Gerard Manley Hopkins, *Further Letters*
      of Gerard Manley Hopkins, edited by Claude Colleer Ab-
      bott (London: Oxford, 1956), pp. 19–20.

88   *"thought it no snatching-matter"* . . . Gerard Manley Hop-
      kins, *Poems and Prose of Gerard Manley Hopkins,* edited
      by W. H. Gardner (Baltimore: Penguin Books, 1953,
      1963), p. 198.

90   *"God must in some way or other make room for Himself"*
      . . . Teilhard de Chardin, *The Divine Milieu* (New York:
      Harper and Row, 1960), p. 89.

91   *"the drug called approval"* . . . Anthony de Mello, *Aware-*
      ness: The Perils and Opportunities of Reality (New York:
      Doubleday, 1990), p. 162.

91   *Jesus "isn't concerned with anyone's opinion"* . . . This is the
      New American Bible's translation of Matthew 22:15–22.

91   *"the politics of illusion"* . . . Wendell Berry, *This Day: Col-*
      lected and New Sabbath Poems (Berkeley, CA: Counter-
      point, 2013), p. 242.

92   *mistake him for the gardener* . . . John 20:11–18.

92   *"Let my prayer be counted as incense"* . . . Psalm 141:2.

93   *"Give joy to your servant, Lord"* . . . Psalm 86:7–8, in *The Liturgy of the Hours According to the Roman Rite,* English translation by the International Commission on English in the Liturgy (New York: Catholic Book Publishing, 1980), volume IV, p. 1009.

93   *It is good "to sing praises to your name"* . . . Psalm 92:1, 3, 4 in *The Liturgy of the Hours According to the Roman Rite,* volume IV, p. 1113.

Part III

95   *"Remember that these things are mysteries"* . . . Flannery O'Connor, *The Habit of Being: Letters Edited and with an Introduction by Sally Fitzgerald* (New York: Farrar, Straus & Giroux, 1979), p. 354.

Chapter 8

98   *"I have no idea where I am going"* . . . Thomas Merton, *Thoughts in Solitude: Meditations on the Spiritual Life and Man's Solitude before God* (New York: Dell, 1961), p. 103.

99   *Our eyes are burning* . . . From the Buddha's "Fire Sermon," quoted in Jack Kornfield, *After the Ecstasy, the Laundry: How the Heart Grows Wise on the Spiritual Path* (New York: Bantam, 2001), p. 65.

100   *"Go from your country"* . . . Genesis 12:1.

101   *Abraham later laughs* . . . Genesis 17:17.

101   *Sarah laughs in joy* . . . Genesis 21:6.

101   *"God asks Abraham to offer him as a human sacrifice"* . . . Genesis 22:1–19.

102   *"The soul is like a wild animal"* . . . Parker Palmer, *Let Your Life Speak: Listening to the Voice of Vocation* (San Francisco: Jossey-Bass, 2004), pp. 7–8.

102   *"Where are you?"* . . . Genesis 3:9, 13.

102   *"Am I my brother's keeper?"* . . . Genesis 4:9.

103   *"Who am I?"* . . . Exodus 3:11.

104   *In the case of the woman at the well* . . . John 4:13–26.

104   *Peter . . . wanting to build booths* . . . Mark 9:5–6, 33–37.

105   *Scripture is a forest* . . . John Henry Newman, *Essay on the Development of Christian Doctrine* (Notre Dame, IN: Notre Dame University Press, 1989), p. 71.

106   *"a broken vessel"* . . . Psalm 31:12.

106   *Everything is "gathered up" in Christ* . . . Ephesians 1:10.

106   *"Who has measured the waters"* . . . Isaiah 40:12.

108   *"Nights and days, bless the Lord"* . . . the New American Bible translation of Daniel 3:71–72, 81, from a long poetic text regarded as canonical by Catholics but not included

in the New Revised Standard Version's translation of Daniel.

109   *God is not to be "investigated"* . . . quoted in Sebastian Brock, *The Luminous Eye: The Spiritual World of Saint Ephrem the Syrian* (Kalamazoo, MI: Cistercian Publications, 1985), p. 65.

109   *"Rebuke your thought"* . . . quoted in Brock, *The Luminous Eye,* p. 69.

109   *"In this quest to seek and find God"* . . . Pope Francis, interview in *America,* September 30, 2013.

Chapter 9

114   *"Never try to get things too clear"* . . . Friedrich von Hügel, *Letters to a Niece* (London: HarperCollins, 1995), p. 8.

114   *"I wanted to be just as certain"* . . . Augustine, *Confessions,* p. 116.

114   *"In your book were written all the days"* . . . Psalm 139:16–18.

115   *Moses wanted to see God* . . . Exodus 33:18–23.

116   *"Jesus is so defined by his faithful obedience"* . . . Luke Timothy Johnson, *The Living Gospel* (London and New York: Continuum, 2004), pp. 180–81.

116   *"eating the bread of anxious toil"* . . . Psalm 127:2.

116   *the seed "sprouts and grows he knows not how"* . . . Mark 4:26–29.

117   *"Between the Idea / and the reality / . . . Falls the Shadow"* . . . T. S. Eliot, "The Hollow Men," in *The Complete Poems and Plays* (New York: Harcourt, Brace, 1971), p. 58.

117   *Jesus at table, in Emmaus* . . . Luke 24:13–35.

118   *"Divine love meets us in this real world"* . . . Ruth Burrows, *The Essence of Prayer* (Mahwah, NJ: HiddenSpring, 2006), p. 81.

120   *"Without giving up hope"* . . . Pema Chodron, *When Things Fall Apart: Heart Advice for Difficult Times* (Boston: Shambhala Publications, 2000), pp. 38–39.

121   *the idea of "indifference"* . . . *The Spiritual Exercises of St. Ignatius*, translated by Anthony Mottola (New York: Doubleday, 1964, 1989), pp. 47–48.

122   *When an idea or a feeling comes from God* . . . William Barry, S.J., *Praying the Truth: Deepening Your Friendship with God through Honest Prayer* (Chicago: Loyola Press, 2012), pp. 13–15. Barry, a Jesuit, is drawing on St. Ignatius.

        Again, see here "Making a Choice of a Way of Life" and "rules" for what Ignatius calls "The Discernment of Spirits," in *The Spiritual Exercises*, Mottola, pp. 81–87 and pp. 129–32.

123   *"The Spirit himself bears witness with our spirit"* . . . Romans 9:16.

124   *"Do not worry about . . . what you will eat" . . .* Matthew 6:25–26.

124   *"I am the Bread of Life" . . .* John 6:35.

Chapter 10

126   *life is "almost indecently eager to evolve eyes" . . .* quoted in Michael Dowd, *Thank God for Evolution: How the Marriage of Science and Religion Will Transform Your Life and Our World* (New York: Viking, 2009), p. 39.

126   *"It takes an entire universe to make an apple pie" . . .* quoted in Dowd, *Thank God for Evolution,* p. 107.

127   *"A thought, a material improvement" . . .* Teilhard de Chardin, *The Divine Milieu* (New York: Harper and Row, 1960), p. 55.

128   *"We serve to complete the work of creation" . . .* Teilhard, *The Divine Milieu,* p. 62.

128   *Before we pray, . . . we should "seek this disposition" . . .* Anthony de Mello, *Wellsprings: A Book of Spiritual Exercises* (New York: Doubleday, 1986), p. 12.

129   *"a little thing" like a nut, a hazelnut . . .* Julian of Norwich, *Showings,* translated and edited by Edmund College, O.S.A., and James Walsh, S.J. (Mahwah, NJ: Paulist Press, 1978), p. 130.

129   *"In those who are making spiritual progress" . . . The Spiritual Exercises of St. Ignatius,* translated by Anthony Mottola (New York: Doubleday, 1964, 1989), p. 134.

130   *"a billion times told lovelier"* . . . "The Windhover," in *Gerard Manley Hopkins: The Complete Poems* (New York: Oxford University Press, 1970), p. 69.

130   *comes the harvest* . . . *"some a hundredfold"* . . . Matthew 13:31–32, 8.

130   *the disciples are filled with "great joy"* . . . Luke 24:50–53.

130   *may "the eyes of your hearts [be] enlightened"* . . . Ephesians 1:18–19.

131   *the one who "fills all things"* . . . Ephesians 4:10.

132   *"Don't think that union lies in being very close to God"* . . . Teresa of Avila, *The Life of St. Teresa*, in *The Collected Works of St. Teresa of Avila*, volume I, p. 398.

134   *"I have said these things to you"* . . . John 15:11.

135   *"When a woman is in labor"* . . . John 16:20–22.

A Note on the Examen

138   *"The first point is to render thanks"* . . . *The Spiritual Exercises of St. Ignatius*, translated by Anthony Mottola (New York: Doubleday, 1964, 1989), pp. 48–49.

140   *In "Making a Choice of a Way of Life," Ignatius* . . . *The Spiritual Exercises of St. Ignatius*, Mottola, pp. 82–87.

140   *In "The Discernment of Spirits," he* . . . *The Spiritual Exercises of St. Ignatius*, Mottola, pp. 129–32.

140　　*As Ignatius says in the "Suscipe," ... The Spiritual Exercises of St. Ignatius*, Mottola, p. 104.

140　　*that we are created to ... The Spiritual Exercises of St. Ignatius*, Mottola, p. 47.

Further Reading

....

On the Examen, Ignatius, and Jesuit Spirituality

For an authoritative translation of the Spanish text of *The Spiritual Exercises*, with a detailed commentary, see *The Spiritual Exercises of Saint Ignatius: A Literal Translation and a Contemporary Reading,* by David Fleming, S.J. (Saint Louis: The Institute of Jesuit Resources, 1978). The translation I prefer, for its readability, and the one I use in this book, is by Anthony Mottola (New York: Doubleday, 1964, 1989).

For more on the history, theology, and practice of the *examen*, see Timothy Gallagher's *The Examen Prayer: Ignatian Wisdom for Our Lives Today* (New York: Crossroad, 2006), and Jim Manney's *A Simple Life-Changing Prayer: Discovering the Power of St. Ignatius Loyola's Examen* (Chicago: Loyola Press, 2011).

James Martin, S.J., explains the *examen* in a clear and readable way in *The Jesuit Guide to (Almost) Everything: A Spirituality for Real Life* (New York: HarperCollins, 2010). This is also a good introduction to *The Spiritual Exercises* as a whole and to the tradition of Jesuit spirituality.

For a brief introduction to prayer in the Jesuit tradition, see William Barry, S.J., *Praying the Truth: Deepening Friendship with God through Honest Prayer* (Chicago: Loyola Press, 2012).

In *When the Well Runs Dry: Prayer beyond the Beginnings* (Notre Dame, IN: Ave Maria Press, 2007), Thomas Greene, S.J., explores what desolation means in the life of prayer.

Two twentieth-century Jesuits are particularly important:

Teilhard de Chardin, S.J., the French paleontologist and theologian, celebrates the sacramental reality of the natural world. See especially *The Divine Milieu* (New York: Harper and Row, 1960).

Anthony de Mello, S.J., a psychotherapist from India, explores the psychology of faith while also sharing stories from different traditions. See especially *Awareness: The Perils and Opportunities of Reality* (New York: Doubleday, 1990).

On Catholic Thought and Spirituality Generally

Ruth Burrows, a Dominican sister from England, writes with uncompromising clarity about the challenges of faith. See *The Essence of Prayer* (Mahwah, NJ: HiddenSpring, 2006), and her analysis of St. Teresa, *Interior Castle Explored: St. Teresa's Teaching on the Life of Deeper Union with God* (Mahwah, NJ: Hidden-Spring, 2007).

Michael Casey, a Trappist monk from Australia, shares the insights of monasticism for laypeople. See, for example, *Seventy-Four Tools for Good Living: Reflections on the Fourth Chapter of Benedict's Rule* (Collegeville, MN: Liturgical Press, 2014).

Dorothy Day's diaries, *The Duty of Delight*, dramatize her inner life over years of service to others (New York: Image Books, 2008, edited by Robert Ellsberg).

Mother Teresa's letters and private writings, *Come Be My Light*, also describe the inner life of faith and service (New York: Doubleday, 2007, edited and with commentary by Brian Kilodiejchuk, M.C.).

Out of the many writings of Thomas Merton, I suggest beginning with his brief *Thoughts in Solitude: Meditations on the Spiritual Life* (New York: Dell, 1961).

Jean Vanier founded the L'Arche communities, where ordinarily-abled people live and work with the developmentally disabled. See *Becoming Human* (Mahwah, NJ: Paulist Press, 1998).

Luke Timothy Johnson's collection of essays, *The Living Gospel* (New York: Bloomsbury Academic, 2004), demonstrates how to read the Scriptures in a way that's both scholarly and faithful.

On Joy

In his Apostolic Exhortation, *The Joy of the Gospel* (New York: Image, 2013), Pope Francis—our first Jesuit Pope—calls us to share the joy we find in the gospel and defines joy in light of the gospel.

Light When It Comes is my response to this call.

In his memoir, *Surprised by Joy: The Shape of My Early Life* (New York: Harcourt, Brace, 1955), C. S. Lewis describes the defining moments of his life as moments of "joy."

On Buddhist Thought and Spirituality

The writing of the American Buddhist monk Pema Chodron is a good introduction to Buddhist spirituality. See, for example, *When Things Fall Apart: Heart Advice for Difficult Times* (Boston: Shambhala, 2000).

See also Jack Kornfield's *After the Ecstasy, the Laundry: How the Heart Grows Wise on the Spiritual Path* (New York: Bantam, 2001).

Poetry

For those attracted to poetry but not sure where to begin, I recommend these books:

Wendell Berry, *This Day: Collected and New Sabbath Poems* (Berkeley, CA: Counterpoint, 2013).

Mary Oliver, *Why I Wake Early* (Boston: Beacon Press, 2004).

William Stafford, *An Oregon Message: Poems* (New York: Harper and Row, 1987).

Acknowledgments

....

The title *Light When It Comes* is from the poem "Simple Talk" by William Stafford, from *The Way It Is: New and Selected Poems*. Copyright ©1987 by William Stafford. It is used here with permission of The Permissions Company, Inc., on behalf of Graywolf Press and Kim Stafford. I am very grateful to Kim Stafford for this, and for our conversation about the book and about his father.

I am very grateful to Brian Doyle for his foreword to this book. I admire him as a believer and I admire him as a writer, and I can't think of anyone I'd rather have associated with my work.

I am very grateful to the fine writers who have written endorsements for the book.

A number of pieces in the book are drawn from homilies I first preached at St. Mary's Catholic Church in Corvallis, Oregon, and I want to thank the people of the parish for their faith, their example, and their support.

Other pieces are based on earlier versions published in the form of poems, and I want to thank the editors of these publications for their encouragement and support, especially Tim Greene, editor of *Rattle*, and my collaborators at Airlie Press, publisher of *The Next Thing Always Belongs*, a book of my poems.

My sincere thanks to Lex Runciman for helping me understand the form of the book; to Richard Wakefield and Catherine Otto, for their thorough and sympathetic reading of the first draft; to Tara Robinson, for her suggestions; to Maggie Anderson, for creating my wonderful website.

My sincere thanks to the editors and designers and staff at Eerdmans press for all they've done to make this book as good as it can be, particularly to the designers of the cover and to Mary Hietbrink for the fine, gentle, very expert advice on the clarity and rhythm of my sentences.

Most of all, my thanks to my superb editor at Eerdmans, Lil Copan, for her encouragement, her rigor, and her clear sense of what I was trying to do. Without her, it can truly be said, this book would not exist.